Salt, Fire,

&

Mango Juice

By Anthony D Hemp

For permissions, contact:
mauihemp808@gmail.com

Photography, Design, and Layout by: Anthony D. Hemp

Cover selection: Leilani F. Hemp

ISBN 979-8-234-03291-1

Printed in the United States of America

For

Chaisley & Leilani

Live wide. Stay curious.

Trust your instincts and don't shrink yourself for anyone.

The world is bigger than fear and kinder than it looks.

You are capable of far more than you'll ever be told.

Dad

Table Of Contents:

Authors Note

This book exists because the man I used to be wasn't going to survive what happened. Maui gave me space. What I became was still my responsibility.

Writing this book forced me to relive moments I had buried for years. There were long nights where I remembered things I had forgotten, and moments I still struggle to read out loud.

Releasing this story into the world was a fear of mine. But avoiding that fear would mean avoiding the truth, and this book only exists because I chose not to do that.

I'm writing this so I don't lose the version of myself that made it through. Writing keeps me honest. If this helps someone else along the way, that's a bonus. The truth is simple. I wrote this to leave behind something real that proves I lived through it.

My life didn't have stability. It was fast, chaotic, and shaped by choices that either pushed me forward or blew everything apart. I learned everything the hard way because I didn't know any other way to live. I loved recklessly, failed more than I want to admit, and spent years moving in survival mode. None of it was graceful, but all of it mattered.

Skateboarding was the one constant I had. From my first day on the island to my last, that board was with me. It carried me through reckless nights, empty roads, grief, silence, and momentum. When everything else fell apart, it gave me movement. It gave me focus. It gave me a way forward when standing still would have swallowed me.

I didn't decide to write this book right away. It happened years later, after I left the island and returned to the mainland. Writing became a way to measure the distance between who I was and who I needed to become, not to celebrate the change, but to understand it.

I never stopped moving toward the best version of myself.

This book is my journey.

I have changed the names of most people in this book and made minor adjustments to protect their privacy. There are no composites.

PART I

COLLAPSE

1

When I was nineteen, I stood in the snow and watched it cover a small casket. It was twenty-six degrees outside. When we opened the church doors to carry him to the limo, giant snowflakes began to fall, slow and heavy. As if the world had shifted to a different pace.

At the cemetery, I froze, staring at the small casket in front of me, unable to hear a single word being said. My body moved on autopilot.

The hardest part was the private viewing, when his mother asked me to help wrap him in his favorite blanket. I lifted him gently and held my son for the last time.

That moment split my life in two.

After the funeral, his mother went to college, and I stayed behind. Our lives were already moving in different directions, but grief pushed them apart faster than I could understand. There was no closure. No long conversation about how we felt. No plan for how to survive what had happened. We just drifted, staying busy enough not to think.

We spoke less as the months passed. Sometimes, in the middle of the night, she would show up and fall asleep without saying much. I never knew if it helped her or hurt her, but it filled a small piece of the emptiness for me.

Eventually, even that stopped.

Drinking became the way I dealt with everything. Sometimes more than drinking.

My family was scattered. My friends were young and lost in their own ways. No one told me to slow down. No one told me to stop. Most nights, there was always another party, another distraction, another reason not to sit still long enough to feel anything.

Eventually, I started losing things. First the apartment. Then my job. Then my vehicle.

I bounced from couch to couch, taking life day by day. Some mornings I woke up not knowing where I was or how I got there. One time I woke up in a woman's dorm room, 366 miles from home. I still don't know how I ended up at BYU.

Time was moving fast. I wasn't.

One night, I was sitting alone on a couch in a dark basement. My eyes were closed, replaying pieces of my childhood like a film I couldn't turn off. That's when the thought showed up. Quiet. Clear. Not loud or chaotic. Just there.

I didn't react to it. I just sat with it.

Then I heard footsteps. Someone came down the stairs. I opened my eyes and saw my cousin Will. He sat down, turned on the TV, and started talking like nothing was wrong. After a while, he looked at me and said, "I'm proud of you, bro."

It didn't land right.

I remember staring at him, trying to understand what he saw that I didn't. Nothing about my life made sense to be proud of.

A few minutes later, my friend Jesse came down the stairs. We talked for a bit. Nothing heavy. But before he left, he paused. "Don't be a weak ass bitch," he said. "Get your head right. Love you, dog." Then he left.

The room went quiet again. But something had shifted. I didn't change overnight. But I started to see how unstable everything had become.

I needed something that felt like mine. Something steady.

So, I went back to work. Paid bills. Did the basics. That's when everything changed.

I might be a father again.

I had already decided I never wanted children again. Not after losing my son. Not with the possibility of going through that kind of loss twice.

But walking away wasn't something I could live with. So, I stayed. Not because it was right. Not because it was healthy. But because there was a chance that child was mine, and that was enough.

We weren't good for each other. That much was clear. There was tension that never really left, trust that never fully existed, and a constant feeling that something wasn't right.

When my daughter came into the world, everything else disappeared. There was no question she was mine. She looked just like me. Nothing else mattered. Those late nights became everything. She knew me. She calmed in my arms. For the first time in a long time, I felt something steady.

Those days I barley slept. My son had died from SIDS, so I woke up constantly to check her breathing, again and again, every night. Fear became routine. But so did purpose.

Eight months later, it fell apart.

One day, she was in my arms every night. The next, she was gone. No goodbye. Just silence. Legal doors closed faster than I knew how to knock on them.

On her first birthday, she spent the day with me. We celebrated. Took pictures. Ate cake. She laughed the way only one-year-olds can, like the world had never disappointed her before.

When the day ended, her mom took her. And that was it. The calls slowed. Messages stopped. Then the silence stayed. There was no conversation. No moment where anything was explained. Just distance growing until it became normal.

Months later, I gathered the few things she had left at my place. Small clothes. Toys. A pair of tiny shoes by the door. I held those shoes longer than I expected to. By the time I saw her again, the little girl who wore them might not remember me.

It felt like I had buried two children.

That was when the real question arrived: Who would I become?

Every corner of my life held memories I couldn't escape. A therapist once told me I carried the stress of a forty-year-old man at twenty. I didn't know how to fix anything. I only knew I couldn't stay where I was.

The noise didn't stop when everything went quiet. It followed me. Things I had heard started to settle in, slowly, until they didn't feel like anyone else's words anymore. They felt like mine. I stopped questioning them. I just carried them.

When a friend told me he had a spare room in Arizona, I didn't hesitate. I left.

That's how I ended up in the desert.

The Mojave night was cold, stars scattered across a sky that didn't care whether I made it out of my twenties. The bonfire cracked in front of us, wild and alive, like I used to feel before everything went quiet inside me.

I didn't come out here for peace. I came because I couldn't stand being alone with the version of myself I had become.

Dalt, Jerry, and I had spent months drifting around Bullhead City, killing time more than we were living it. This was supposed to be our last night together, one more fire, one more cheap beer, one more round of pretending we weren't all a little lost.

As the sun dropped behind the jagged desert mountains, the sky went from orange to ash. Someone threw a pallet on the fire, sparks shooting into the dark like something trying to escape. For a few minutes, the laughter felt real. For a few minutes, I could almost believe I was okay.

The laughter carried on, but it never reached the part of me that needed it. I wasn't feeling normal. I was faking it, the same way I had been for the last year. I kept waiting for something inside me to come back to life, but all I felt was the darkness.

Then Jerry stood up and said he was moving back to Lahaina. He mentioned there was a spare room, in case any of us ever made it out that way. He meant it as a throwaway offer, but it hit me harder than it should have. I didn't know why at the time, but the idea of leaving everything behind felt like the first real lifeline I'd heard in months.

The night went quiet right before the shots. When the bullets cracked through the desert, I froze. For a second, I didn't move at all. I wasn't shocked. I wasn't scared. I just felt this heavy thought settle in: maybe this is how it ends for me. Quick, random, and forgettable.

Instinct finally kicked in, and I ran with the others, legs scrambling up the hill while my brain stayed stuck on that one thought. I checked myself behind a boulder, waiting to feel blood, waiting for pain.

My hands were shaking, but I couldn't tell if it was fear or habit. I felt embarrassed that I was still alive, like I'd failed at something I hadn't admitted I was hoping for. My mind was quiet, no panic, no prayer. I didn't feel relief. I felt exposed. Like life had looked straight at me and decided I wasn't done yet.

When the shooting stopped, we stayed hidden until the silence felt real. Then the shock hit us, and we started laughing, like people do when they don't know what else to do. When we finally went down, we saw the truth. A box of ammo had been buried in the fire pit. Some jerk before us had covered it with dirt. The heat caused the rounds to go off on their own. Nobody was aiming at us. The desert wasn't trying to kill us. We were just idiots who got lucky.

I stared at the coals as something shifted inside me. For the first time in a year, I was awake. Ever since the day I watched snow cover my son's casket, a part of me believed it should have been me instead. I didn't fear death after that. I feared life.

On the drive back toward town, the desert rolled past in silence. That's when my mind did what it always did when things got quiet. It went to the places I avoided. I wondered where my daughter was. I didn't know what she looked like anymore. I didn't know what her voice sounded like. I didn't know if she ever asked about me, or if my name had already been erased from her life. There was no grave to visit. No ending to stand in front of. Just the knowledge that she was out there somewhere, growing up without me.

That was the weight I was carrying when the desert went quiet again.

2

Three weeks later, that whisper became a plane ticket I couldn't afford and a fear I couldn't escape.

Airplanes.
Fucking airplanes.

Trapped inside a metal tube with only gravity and fate between me and the ocean. My worst nightmare. Elevators and planes are two places where you lose control. And now I was willingly stepping into one.

People laugh at that.
But it was never about the plane.

I stepped onto the plane with ninety dollars in my pocket and a skateboard under my arm, not knowing I was walking away from the boy I had been. There was a darkness close behind. I hoped the engines could outpace it, that maybe it would lose my trail in the clouds.

At the time, I thought I was leaving because I had nothing left to lose. What I didn't know was that the journey would decide what kind of man I would become.

When the wheels left the ground, panic detonated in my chest. My heart felt caged and frantic, a hummingbird beating against bone. Every instinct screamed to get out. But there was nowhere left to run. I'd already been doing that for too long.

Why did I get on this airplane?

I was escaping. That's the truth of it. Back home, I felt smothered, like everyone had already decided who I was and nothing I said mattered anymore. A bad father. A bad person. After a while, I stopped trying to explain myself. I just let them keep the story they wanted and walked away from the whole place.

But that didn't mean I knew what I was doing. I wasn't flying toward a fresh start. I was trying to breathe again, trying to get far enough away from the noise and the memories that I could hear my own thoughts.

I stared out the window as the world fell away, cities shrinking into tiny constellations shaped by people who still had reasons to stay. I wasn't sure I belonged among them. The cabin dimmed, just darkness, engine roar, and the vibration from the window against my forehead.

Before boarding, I'd sent a couple of messages. Nothing heavy. No speeches. Just the kind of words you send when you don't want to worry anyone. Dalt. Jesse. For them, it was a see-you-later. For me, it felt final. I didn't need them to understand it. I just needed to know I'd said something before disappearing.

Fear wasn't a stop sign. It was a fucking mirror.

I didn't picture Maui. I didn't imagine a place to land, a job, a room, or a version of myself waiting on the other side. My mind didn't go that far. It stopped at the flight. The future felt unnecessary. Not frightening. Just irrelevant. I wasn't running toward anything. I was letting momentum decide what came next.

I wasn't afraid the plane would go down. I was afraid it wouldn't. Afraid that I would step off alive and have to figure out what came after, when I had already let go of wanting anything at all.

Hours passed. I didn't sleep. Fear kept me awake. Guilt too. But underneath all that noise was something worse, a small flicker of possibility I didn't trust.

When the pilot announced our descent into Kahului, relief slammed into me like a wave, but it didn't wash anything away. It revealed the truth. If I made it to Maui, I'd have to face the life waiting for me there.

Then the lights of the island appeared, scattered across a black ocean, isolated, unreachable, final. There was no going back from this. No running. No hiding. If darkness wanted to consume me, it would have to do it here.

The aircraft kissed the runway. Tires screamed. So did every nerve in my body. Stepping off the plane, the tropical air wrapped around me, warm, salty, sweet.

It should have been an arrival. Instead, it was a confrontation. This place didn't glow for me. It stared me down. People seemed lighter, smiling, laughing, untouched by the weight I carried. I felt like a fraud the second my feet hit Hawaiian ground. But here I was. One-way. No plan. No parachute.

The plane door opened.
Warm salt air rushed in.

Maui wasn't just a destination.
It was a challenge.

PART II
SEDUCTION

3

I landed on Maui with next to nothing: ninety bucks, a skateboard, and a phone number for a guy named Michael, a friend of Jerry's. We'd talked a couple of times before the flight, enough for me to gamble on trusting him.

Through the crowd of *Aloha* shirts and rolling luggage, I spotted him holding a sign that said "Hemp." "You must be Anthony," he grinned. "Aloha, welcome to paradise."

Paradise.

The word didn't sit right in my stomach. I didn't feel like someone who deserved paradise.

I tossed my board and bag into his trunk and got into the car. We headed west toward Lahaina, a town older than America, older than the version of myself I'd been dragging around for years. I didn't know it yet, but this place would strip me bare before rebuilding me. Maui would hold me for nearly seven years.

The drive hugged the coastline, black ocean on one side, ancient mountains towering on the other. Michael talked fast, laughed loudly, and was full of energy, which I couldn't remember ever having. Somehow, he made the ride feel easy, like crossing an ocean wasn't something insane people did on ninety bucks and panic.

Close to midnight, we pulled into Lahaina. The town was still, half asleep, lit by streetlamps and moonlight. No people, no traffic, just the slow rhythm of waves crashing into the seawall. Even empty, Front Street felt alive, like stories were tucked into every corner, waiting.

When we reached the Wahikuli apartments, nerves hit me. I had actually made it. My room was bare, just an air mattress and salt air drifting through the windows. The place was honest. Almost too honest. Like the island wasn't fooled by whatever mask I thought I still had on.

After Michael left, I sat outside on the *lanai* under two massive mango trees. I was borrowing a life that didn't belong to me yet.

Michael and Jerry had handed me a key and a place to land without hesitation. I wasn't used to kindness that didn't come with strings.

The night was calm, but I didn't relax into it. I stayed alert without trying to, like a part of me didn't believe this could last. Even when I finally lay down, sleep came heavy and fast, but the guard stayed up. My body was out cold. My mind stayed watchful. I'd been carrying myself for too long to set everything down at once.

The moon reflected off the ocean, turning everything silver and soft. The calm was almost suspicious. A kind of calm I didn't trust. A calm that made me wonder what was coming next.

Stillness wasn't something I was used to. It usually meant the hit was coming. For a long moment, I just stood there, breathing air that felt like it belonged to a different life.

There were mangos everywhere covering the ground. I'd never seen a mango tree before, and now I was living under two of them. I grabbed a mango picka leaning nearby and went searching like it was my new mission. The red dirt was warm beneath my feet, soft and almost glowing in the moonlight. The fruit hung golden-orange on the branches. I pulled a few down and tore into them, juice dripping down my arms and face. It was *ono*, wild, and pure. First thing I had eaten straight from the earth. That tree became a ritual before I even realized it.

Later, lying on the air mattress in the quiet, something strange crept in. Relief, a tiny breath of it. But it came with distance. Distance from my family, from everything I'd ever known.

Maui was another world. Salvation or abandonment, I couldn't tell.

Morning came bright and loud. From the *lanai*, I saw the islands of Molokai and Lanai floating in the distance like something drawn into existence just for me. For the first time in my life, I was staring at the ocean. I had never seen it before. The air was thick, sweet, alive. I drank my coffee and listened as the old sugar cane train whistled across the yard, tourists waving like I was already part of the island.

Michael showed up not long after. "Let's cruise," he said. We crossed the street to Wahikuli Beach Park, locals call it Sandbox. I kicked off my slippahs and ran barefoot into the sand. The world slowed the second my feet touched it. The waves vibrated through me, like the island was introducing itself. I sprinted into the water and dove into the blue. Floating there, staring at the sky, I was weightless, like gravity forgot I existed. For a moment, I wasn't haunted. I wasn't guilty. I just was.

I hadn't felt weightless like that in years. I had forgotten what it even felt like to exist without pressure on my chest. I had spent so long believing I was a nobody, a failure, that feeling good felt wrong. I couldn't shake the idea that I hadn't earned a moment like this.

The sun burned my shoulders. Salt dried on my lips.
Lungs full. My body was remembering how to be alive before my mind.

Then something bumped my leg. My heart dropped out of my chest. A massive *honu* drifted by, slow, ancient, calm, three feet of prehistoric silence. I laughed, half from shock, half from awe. When I got out, Michael shook his head. "Rookie," he said.

That first day, the ocean gave me a moment clean enough to keep breathing. Somewhere across the ocean, I had left behind a darkness. For the first time in a long time, I felt space.

4

Michael and I left the beach and headed toward Kihei, but first, he wanted me to see Front Street in the daylight. "Gotta see it proper," he said.

Driving into Lahaina felt like sliding into another universe. The first stretch of road passed oceanfront houses, real ones, multi-million-dollar homes. I had never been near anything that polished. People who lived in places like that didn't run from their lives the way I had. They didn't land on islands with ninety bucks and a skateboard.

We rolled past a small neighborhood and a beach locals call Baby Beach. I didn't know it then, but a year later I'd be living right there. I couldn't see the future, and I barely trusted the ground under my feet.

At the edge of town stood two massive mango trees, branches heavy with fruit. A sign on the fence warned, "*Ey, No Mango Picka's*!" Every time I passed by, it took effort not to stop. You could smell them from across the street, sweet and tempting. They reminded me of the mango trees outside my apartment, like the island was repeating something I wasn't ready to understand.

Next door, four tall coconut trees leaned over the seawall, casting long shadows across the road. Lahaina felt alive. Tourists wandering with shaved ice, surfers heading toward breakwall, couples holding hands, locals cruising by like they'd been born with sunshine in their veins.

The air carried everything at once. Salt, grilled food drifting out of open restaurants, hints of cologne and perfume as people passed by. Shops, small studios, churches, and old buildings lined the streets, each one holding a piece of something that had been there long before me.

You could feel it without anyone saying it.

Out past the shoreline, boats moved in and out of the harbor while cruise ships and military vessels sat heavy on the horizon. Surfers dotted the water at breakwall, waiting, watching, then disappearing into waves like it was second nature.

Toward the end of town, Michael pointed ahead. "There it is, the banyan tree." At first, I thought it was a grove. "Which one?" I asked. He laughed. "All of them. That's one tree."

Up close, it didn't feel real. Trunks spreading outward, branches rooting into the ground as if it had grown itself into a small forest to stay standing. One tree pretending to be many. Or maybe many roots pretending to be one.

Standing under it felt like standing inside a cathedral made of roots. The tree had figured out how to stay. How to change without leaving. How to survive by becoming more than one thing at once.

The idea of permanence didn't scare me. It felt comforting in a way I couldn't fully explain. But it came with a low, unfamiliar anxiety. I couldn't remember the last time I'd belonged anywhere long enough to grow roots of my own, and I didn't yet know what that was supposed to feel like.

Either way, it held something I recognized.

Michael told me it was more than 150 years old. "It's the most beautiful tree I've ever seen," I said, and I meant it.

For a moment, staring at that tangle of strength and age, I wondered if maybe I could root here too. That tree was the first time Maui showed me what staying might look like. But the moment passed quickly.

Michael kept driving, pointing out old haunts, childhood spots, and places he'd gotten into trouble. I could hear nostalgia in his voice, the kind you earn by belonging to a place.

He belonged here.

I didn't. Not yet.

I didn't trust kindness yet. Every open smile felt temporary, like it came with an expiration date I just couldn't see. I was waiting for the island to reject me the way places and people always had, quietly at first, then all at once. Part of me believed belonging was something other people earned by staying still, not something given to someone who arrived with ninety dollars and no plan. So, I kept distance, even while everything around me kept reaching out. Lahaina was bright, humming, and connected. Deep down, I expected rejection.

Still, that banyan tree stayed with me.

Maybe islands didn't judge the same way people did. Maybe they just watched. Maybe, if you stayed long enough, they figured out where to plant you.

To reach Kihei, you cross the pali, a winding road carved into jagged cliffs. Black lava rock towered on one side, the ocean falling away forever on the other. It felt like driving along the edge of the world.

We pulled into the lookout, a cool breeze sweeping across the cliffs, carrying ocean mist and something ancient. Up there, everything was visible. Islands blurred in the haze, boats dragging white streaks in the blue water, whales breaching like moving mountains, cargo ships crossing the horizon. The ocean stretched on forever, its surface alive and restless.

Standing there, I realized I could disappear here. The world wouldn't even flinch. That thought felt both terrifying and safe. I was just a dot on something vast.

We drove into Kihei, flat, warm, sunbaked. Resorts, shops, garages, and industrial buildings lined the streets. The radio station sat upstairs in a small building that smelled like coffee, dust, and old electricity. For someone who loved music, it felt like stepping into a temple.

Inside, walls were stacked with CDs, reels, and tangled cables. Michael slid into the booth, flipped switches, and started recording commercial breaks. His voice deepened into something familiar, the radio voice I'd heard before, without knowing it belonged to the guy driving me around. Watching him, I realized you had to love this job to survive it. He did. He belonged here in a way I didn't yet understand, and I wasn't sure I ever would.

After his session, we hit the road again, the pali glowing silver under the full moon. Island vibes, a friend who spun songs for a living, the randomness of it all hit me at once. My life had twisted into something unrecognizable.

That night, I slept hard. The waves crashed against the shore outside my window. The noise wasn't noise anymore. It was comfort. I wondered if I was allowed to feel it, or if the island was giving me one calm breath before it broke me open.

5

The first month on Maui was mostly spent alone. Jerry had been sent off-island for work before I arrived, leaving me with an empty house. I explored Lahaina, walked Front Street, and spent hours wandering the beaches. In between, I filled out job applications around town, trying to figure out how long ninety dollars and luck could realistically last.

Most days, I skateboarded everywhere. Skateboarding had been my world since I was 14. Skate videos were at their peak, and clips from Maui would show up in videos like Transworld. I had already seen parts of Lahaina before ever stepping foot on the island.

The skateboard world was one of the few places I had always earned respect. It didn't matter where you came from or what you had been through. If you could skate, people knew it immediately. It was the one skill I carried that nobody could deny.

Eventually, someone pointed me toward the Lahaina skatepark. It was only about a ten-minute skate from the apartment, smooth concrete, bowls, rails, stairs, and sunshine. The kind of park skaters dream about. I ended up spending countless hours there over the years. It gave my days structure. Wake up. Explore. Skate. Look for work. Repeat. It helped quiet my mind.

Jerry returned to the island, a little over a month after I landed. The first thing he showed me was the road to Hana. If you spend any time on Maui, someone will eventually tell you the same thing. The Road to Hana isn't just a drive. It's an experience.

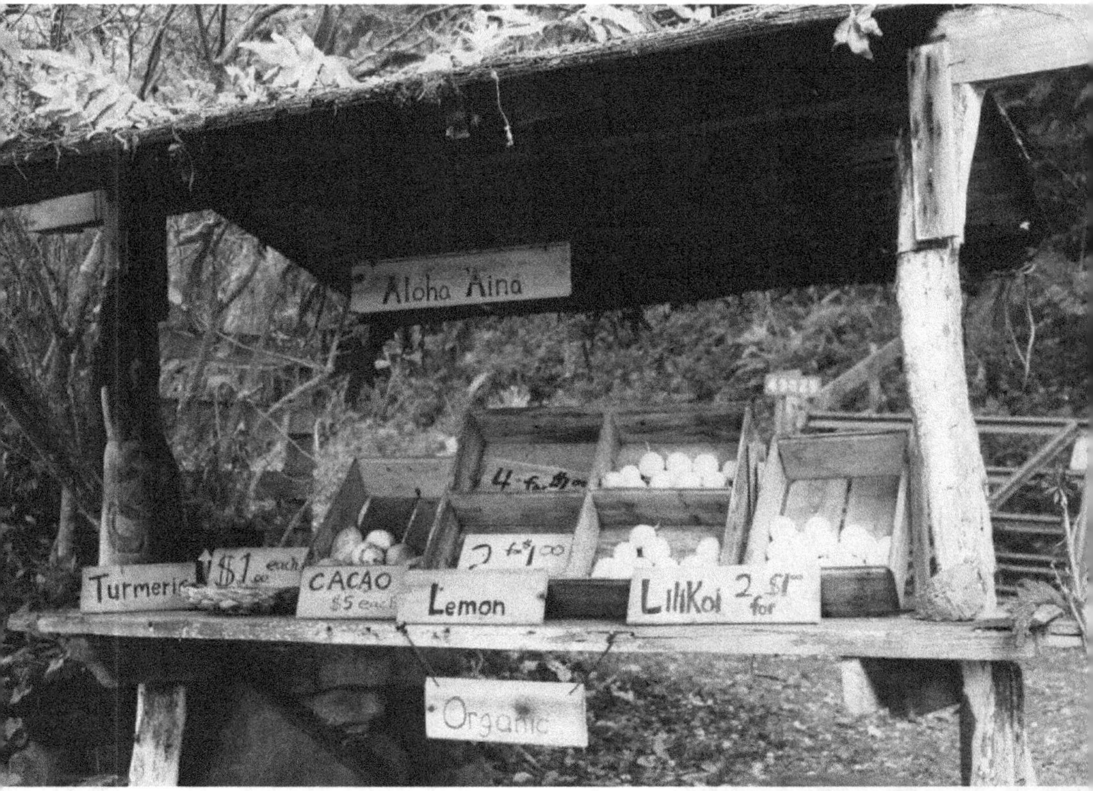
Aloha 'Aina
Turmeric
$1.00 each
CACAO
$5 each
Lemon
2 for $1.00
LiliKoi 2 for $1
Organic

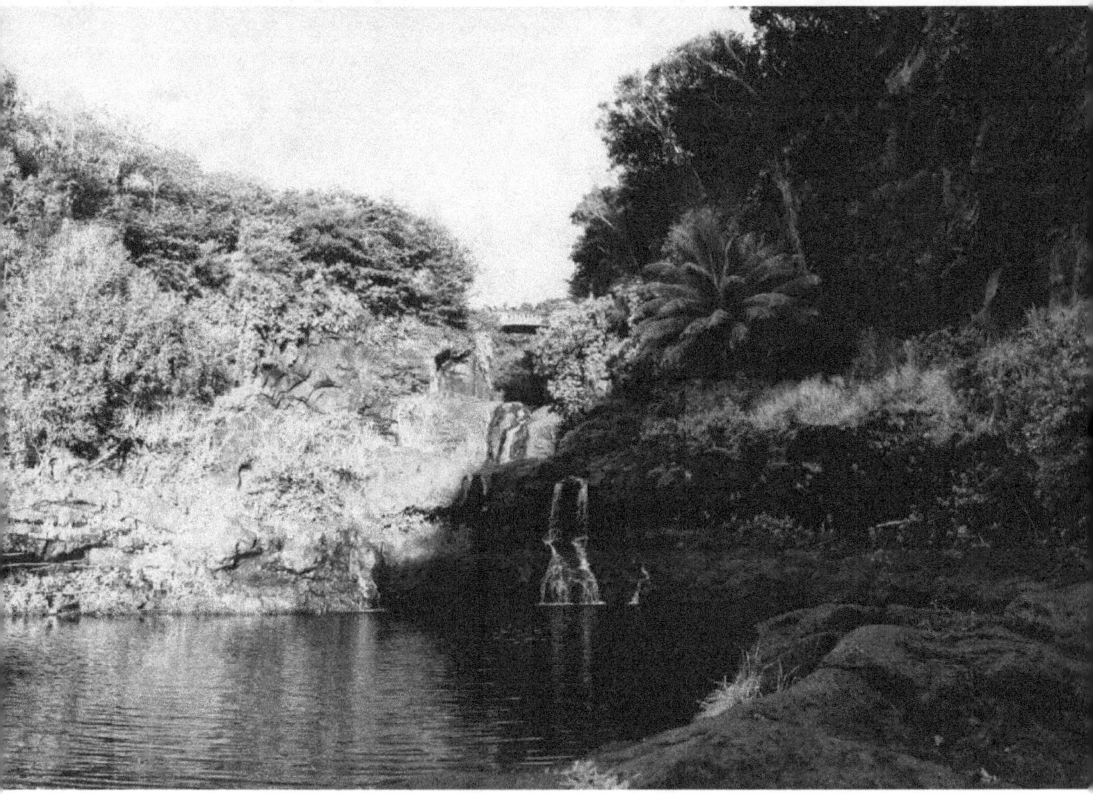

West Maui is dry, almost desert-like, but Hana is a completely different world. Rainy, dense, and green with bamboo forests and waterfalls.

On the way, we passed through the town of Paia. The windows stayed down. Cool jungle air moved through the car, thick with the smell of ginger plants and wet earth. Every corner revealed another stretch of green so dense it felt unreal.

Over a hundred single-lane bridges wound through the jungle, some hiding waterfalls behind them. Fruit stands appeared at the ends of driveways with small wooden boxes left out for money, running entirely on trust.

About an hour in, we stopped at Braddah Hut's BBQ. Best plate lunch I had ever tasted in my life. Onolicious.

From there, we drove to Hamoa Beach, famous for body-surfing. I had never body-surfed before. The first wave folded me in half and slammed me into the sand. By the fifth wave, I learned to dive under and rise behind it. The ocean doesn't allow you to fake courage.

After that, we made our way to the Seven Sacred Pools. A tall bridge stood where water plunged into the pools below. It was my first waterfall. Actually, my first dozen.

The roar of the falls and the ocean beyond made it feel like I was standing inside nature's heartbeat. Standing there, one thought crossed my mind. If my daughter ever came to Maui, this is where I would bring her first.

Jerry climbed a forty-foot ledge and yelled, “Hell yeah!” before jumping. Then it was my turn. I stood there for ten minutes arguing with fear. It wasn’t the height.

Before I jumped, I hesitated. Not because I was afraid of the water, but because I felt everything behind me tug once more. The years I had lived. The weight I had been carrying. The darkness I knew too well. I didn’t look back at anything I could see. I just took a second to acknowledge it. Then I made a quiet decision. I wasn’t going to keep facing backward. Whatever came next, I would meet it head-on.

I went.

The fall punched the breath out of me. The water hit me clean. When I surfaced, I was smiling.

The drive back felt different at night. Headlights cut through tunnels of bamboo while rain drifted through the jungle air. At one point, a barefoot hitchhiker stepped out of the forest with his thumb out. He said he worked on a *pakalolo* farm down the road. We gave him a ride.

When he hopped out, he handed me a little pakalolo. "Mahalo," he said before disappearing back into the darkness.

Back in Lahaina, the night still felt alive. We stopped for pizza at Dollies in Kahana before heading down to DT Fleming Beach Park.

The sand was still warm from the day. A group of girls was sitting in the sand near the shoreline. I asked to joined them, got jag, ate pizza, and laughed while the waves rolled in behind us. We are still friends to this day.

The island vibrated in my chest that night. I didn't know yet how bright Maui could burn before it burned back. Not all the fear was gone. Fear never disappears that quickly. But it wasn't steering me anymore.

Salt dried on my skin. My mind was silent. I slept hard that night.

6

Finding work turned out to be the easy. The turnover rate on Front Street was high. So, when a spot opened at a small shop a block off the strip, I grabbed it.

My first project felt unreal: wrapping motorcycles for a new restaurant called Fleetwoods on Front Street. They were putting a burger on the menu, paired with a limited-edition motorcycle signed by Mick. My job was to wrap the motorcycles with the decals.

On my third day, my boss walked in and told us to take the day off. "Work perk," he said. He'd rented two boats. The guys from work, Zach, Matsu, and I, rode out to Molokini Crater, a half-sunken volcano rising out of the ocean like a broken crown. It was my first time on a boat, my first time piloting one, my first time snorkeling. Sharks glided under me like shadows with weight. Dolphins sliced through the blue glass. Tropical fish flickered like painted sparks. Floating on my back, staring at the sky, I thought, I'm so damn glad I got on that plane. Even then, a part of me whispered, this can't be real.

A month later, I learned what *haole* meant. Locals tossed it at my boss constantly, in the shop, on job sites. It didn't take long to figure out he'd earned it. The guy was shady, no Aloha in him.

After a big job, I showed up to get paid. The place was empty. Locked. He'd taken the truck, the money, and disappeared. No paycheck. No goodbye.

I told myself it didn't matter, that work would always come, and on Maui it usually did. I didn't slow down long enough to ask what would happen if the luck ran out, or if I'd built anything that could hold without it. It was easier to keep moving than to test whether I could stand still.

I started busing tables at a well-known chain restaurant. It was Rock and Roll, open windows, ocean breeze, guitars on the walls, bartenders with mohawks taller than my beer glass. Live shows on the weekends, and employees got in for free.

I had only been there a month when another employee asked if I wanted to take some shifts at another restaurant. A Bar and Grill on the Kaanapali golf course, just a short skate from my house. I played golf all my life and love the game, so working at a restaurant on a renowned course was exciting.

This was a time I really started meeting people from all over the world every day. People took me out, invited me on trips, and I even attended a few weddings.

One day during a shift at the golf course, my boss pulled me aside. "You like basketball?" he asked. "Hell yeah. Sports in general," I replied. He handed me two front-row tickets to the Maui Invitational and told me to clock out.

Courtside seats. Three college games. I sat there half the time shaking my head, wondering how a guy who had landed on the island with ninety dollars and a skateboard ended up watching college basketball from the front row.

When the games ended, I skated home while the day cooled off around me. I felt a strange mix of adrenaline and disbelief, as life suddenly started happening faster than I could keep up with.

Maui continued doing that to me. Moments would appear out of nowhere, things that didn't make sense if I stopped and tried to analyze them. So, I stopped trying. I just accepted them and kept moving.

A few days later, the ocean was glowing orange in the late afternoon light when my phone rang. Michael McCartney. "Howz it? You working?" he asked. "Off till tomorrow." I said. "Shoots. I'm coming to grab you. We're going to see some live music." He shouted.

We pulled up to the venue, and I saw the name glowing on the marquee. Bonnie Raitt. My mother and grandmother used to blast her songs through the house on cleaning days. Seeing her live felt like stumbling into childhood through a side door.

I could already hear the music drifting into the street from the parking lot. The bass thumped through the wooden walls while people spilled out onto the sidewalk, laughing and shouting over the sound of the band inside. When we walked in, the place was packed.

She must've been pushing seventy, but when she walked onstage, hair big, rhinestones catching every light, she was pure fire. The crowd was full of old-timers, tourists, locals, everyone moving to the same heartbeat. Maui had a way of bringing people together.

After the show, Michael led us backstage. Velvet drapes, bowls of snacks, soft lights, and a handful of people. One woman stood out instantly. Clutching a CD so tight her knuckles were white. Eyes wide, frantic, pacing as if her whole future depended on that moment. The second Bonnie walked in, the woman lunged forward. "Bonnie! Please! Listen to my demo. Please listen to it!" Security stepped in fast. "Ma'am, how did you get back here?" She ignored them, voice cracking, "I'm your next big thing!" Real groupie-level meltdown. They finally got her out, her pleas echoing down the hall.

When things settled, Bonnie made her way around the room, greeting everyone, grounded and warm, exactly the kind of woman she sounded like on the records I grew up hearing. When she got to me, I told her my name. She smiled and said, "I'll never forget that one."

I left that night feeling like my soul had been tuned. The next morning, I stepped back into work. But something in me had shifted. More aware. Like every conversation, every person, every breeze meant something.

7

Every good thing Maui gave me was accompanied by a shadow, a quiet voice reminding me it could all vanish the moment I revealed my true self. The feeling seemed to root from the loss I hadn't let go of.

By then, my circle was expanding, co-workers, locals, tourists who'd become friends for a week, then disappear back home. I was experiencing cultures, foods, local slang, and discovering new parts of myself.

Before I knew it, Christmas came. No snow. No cold. Santa wore board shorts and sang "*shoots, bruddah, cuz.*" Every Christmas prior, I had experienced a winter wonderland. Usually, when winter came, I would slip into a dark depression. Not this year. Time moved differently in paradise, and this year, summer never ended.

I started losing touch with people back home, which was necessary. I couldn't grow if I kept one foot on the mainland. But the distance felt sharp. Part of me wondered if anyone even noticed how far away I'd become.

Not long after that, I had my most haole moment on the island. One afternoon, the tsunami alarms went off. I had seen the news earlier that week. They said one might be coming. When the sirens started echoing across town, my brain immediately filled in the rest. Images from Japan flashed in my head, waves swallowing streets, cars floating like toys, entire neighborhoods disappearing in seconds. I stepped outside and looked toward the ocean. Everything looked calm. Too calm. That somehow made it worse.

So, I started walking. Then, jogging uphill. Heart racing. Mind sprinting faster than my legs. I passed aunties and uncles standing in their yards, relaxed, talking story like it was any other day. Meanwhile, I was mentally preparing for the end of the world.

Eventually, I called Jerry to ask if I should actually be worried. He couldn't stop laughing. It was just another Maui day.

Standing there afterward, catching my breath, I had to laugh at myself. I realized how tightly wound I still was, how quickly my mind jumped to worst-case scenarios. I was still living in survival mode, even in paradise.

New Year's came, and my younger brother Bird asked if he could visit. He said he needed a breath of fresh air. So, he got on a plane and headed for Maui.

His first morning, I took him to Sandbox. It felt right for his first time in the ocean to happen in the same place mine did. Something about that mattered to me.

Bird stood at the edge for a moment, said a quiet prayer, and jumped straight in. I gave him snorkel gear and watched him start to relax in the water. When I got out and sat on the beach, an uncle we'd been *talking story* with suddenly yelled, "Honu!" towards Bird.

Bird had no idea what that meant. I told him it was a turtle. He turned just in time to come face to face with it, massive, slow, ancient. He exploded out of the water, ran straight across the surface, and didn't stop until he hit dry sand.

The uncle and I were laughing so hard we cried. Bird kept saying he thought turtles were supposed to be the size of his hand. "Rookie," I told him. That was the moment I understood what Michael must've felt when he first showed me the island.

Watching my brother that day, something sat differently in my chest. I was responsible for how someone else met it. I noticed myself paying closer attention, scanning the water, listening for things I hadn't before.

A few weeks later, I took Bird to Hana. We stopped at waterfalls, fruit stands, and let the road do what it does. We showed him body-surfing at Hamoa Beach before heading to Seven Sacred Pools. When it came time to jump, Bird didn't hesitate the way I had. Watching him experience the same peace and beauty I had felt strange. Like seeing the island for the first time again.

Bird hadn't planned on staying too long. Four weeks on the island, and off he was. His time on Maui was short, but it was enough to change him.

Years later, when we talked about it, he told me he missed the sunsets most. I believe he's right.

Soon after Bird left, Dalt flew out. He was chasing something. Bird, Dalt, and I grew up together. We were blood *ohana.* Like Bird. Like me. Dalt flew at night and had never seen the ocean. His first time would be the same place as ours. Sandbox.

That mattered. The same water. The same first step in. Something about that tied the three of us together in a way words don't fully explain. To this day, it still carries weight between us.

Dalt didn't have an Honu moment like Bird and I did, but he swam farther out than either of us on his first day. I remember watching him and thinking, *damn... he's braver than I was.*

When Dalt arrived, he was like me, work came first. Before he landed, I'd already finished my two-week notice at both jobs. I told him we could work wherever he wanted.

On a solo hike his first day, Dalt googled the *best restaurant in Lahaina.* Fleetwoods on Front Street showed up first.

Inspired by Anthony Bourdain, he walked in and told them he had an interview with the chef.

He didn't.

The chef came out confused. Dalt did what we do best. He stayed calm, talked his way through it, and made it real. Then he waited for the call.

While he waited to hear back, Dalt and I spent a lot of time walking the old sugar cane tracks behind the house. They were quieter than the road, winding through tall grasses and coconut trees, a peaceful way to come and go without seeing many people.

One afternoon we came across a younger local guy named Maka in a small clearing surrounded by thick greenery. He had a few fighting roosters with him. Over time on the islands, I'd run into plenty of people where this was simply part of the culture, whether I agreed with it or not. We talked story for a bit, and before we left Maka sold Dalt a used skateboard for forty bucks. Dalt hadn't brought one with him to Maui, so that became his first board on the island.

A few nights later we were down the road from the house messing around in an empty parking lot, skating under the streetlights. A guy about our age walked by and stopped to watch us for a while. After a minute he asked if he could see Dalt's board. Something about the way he asked didn't sit right with me, so when he reached for it, I grabbed it first and rolled away on it.

We talked for a minute before finally letting him take a look. That's when he told us the board was actually his and that Maka had taken it. Before we could process what he was saying, he snatched it and took off running. Dalt and I just stood there for a second, stunned, before we started laughing.

We bought a stolen skateboard.

A few minutes later, the guy drove past in the back of a *yota* with a bunch of friends, board in hand, already halfway down the road. Back on the mainland, we probably would've chased him down. But Maui had started changing the way I reacted to things. Instead of getting angry, we just laughed about it and kept skating.

Maui had a strange way of slowing things down like that. Even when something went wrong, it didn't feel like the end of the world.

A few days later, we were at a skimboarding competition in Kaanapali when Dalt's phone rang. Not only was he hired, but I was too. The same place I'd wrapped motorcycles months earlier.

Fleetwoods on Fronts Street was a blessing. Two stories tall with a rooftop bar and VIP rooms. The kitchen was spotless, brand new, with stainless steel everywhere. The kind of place that made you want to work harder just to belong. Mick kept a drum set on the main floor, and the rooftop looked out over Front Street, and the ocean. Every night at sunset, someone blew a conch shell while the sky turned gold.

The chef ran a tight ship and taught me more about food than any job before it. Dalt and I went from food runners to professionals in no time. We learned how to shuck oysters, plate desserts, create under pressure, and talk to celebrities without turning into fanboys.

The strange thing about famous people is that after a while, you realize they're usually chasing the same thing everyone else is. Normal. A normal conversation. A normal night out. Someone talking to them like a person instead of a headline. Once I understood that, everything changed. We met Stevie Nicks, and watched Mick play the drums many times.

Real life.

Every day, there was a family-style meal for employees. Dalt and I made it whenever we could, sometimes crossing paths mid-shift, me clocking out as he clocked in. The place felt like ohana. And for two guys who had spent a long time feeling like outsiders, that mattered more than we admitted.

It felt like I was building something instead of just surviving. It was the good life.

One night, I *pau* work and ran into Michael on Front Street. He invited me to get frozen yogurt with a quiet friend of his. The guy and I talked about mountain lions in Wyoming, gators in Florida, and life on the road. He joked that there were T-shirts in his luggage older than me.

People kept staring. Whispering. Smiling. I ignored it. Before he left, the man shook my hand and said, "Mahalo for a great conversation." Then he told me his name.

Michael McDonald, from the Doobie Brothers.

I laughed the whole skate home.

Maui had jokes.

8

It wasn't long before life settled into a rhythm. Work, skate, adventure, repeat.

Dalt and I rode everywhere on our boards. No car. No TV. No real plan. We often spent sunsets in front of the Amida Buddha at the Lahaina Jodo Mission. The two of us had long shared an interest in Buddhist philosophy. We'd walk the grounds, sit quietly, and meditate when it felt right. Nothing forced. Just small moments of balance, we never felt the need to explain.

Most nights after shifts, we ended up at Spanky's Riptide. We'd play pool and talk story to whoever wandered through. Then we'd skateboard home. Front Street was quiet by then, the ocean close enough to hear. Sometimes we ate pavement, laughed it off, and kept going.

We loved bombing Lahaina Luna Road. A long hill starting near the high school, cutting straight down across the highway to Front Street. Our wheels would heat up until they smelled like melting rubber. One wrong move and it's over. Letting go until gravity made the decisions gave us a sense of control.

One night stuck with me. We'd worked a morning shift and spent the evening skateboarding between a few spots, eventually landing at Spanky's. A couple of women joined us at the pool table. Conversations stacked on top of each other.

Everything felt light, connected, effortless. We rolled out around two in the morning, laughing, boards under our arms. As we passed a group of workers dumping trash in another restaurant's shirts, we yelled, "Fleetwoooods!" as we flew by. It cracked us up.

By the edge of downtown, we were cooked. We stepped off our boards and walked. As we passed the "*Ey no mango pickas*" house, a man appeared out of the dark. Light-skinned, bearded, wearing a sharp suit. "Mind if I walk and talk with you?" he asked. "Shoots," we said.

It didn't feel strange. It felt expected. For fifteen minutes, we walked side by side, taking turns speaking. By the time we reached home, he said his goodbyes and disappeared back into the night.

Dalt and I talked about it then, and years later. Neither of us remembers everything that was said. Only the feeling that it mattered. We were exactly where we were supposed to be. Maybe it was just a guy at two in the morning on an empty street. Whether it meant something or nothing didn't change the fact that we were still responsible for the lives we walked back into.

By then, Dalt, Jerry, and I had started to know our neighbors. Just enough. One afternoon, the ice broke. Dalt was watering the garden on the lanai when the neighbor stepped outside and called out, "*Cheehoo.*" He tossed a paper ball my way. I caught it. Inside was a handful of pakalolo. Later, we learned

Raj was a retired Brazilian soccer player who'd come to Maui with his sister.

That evening, Dalt and I set up horseshoes under the mango tree. We'd found a few sets around the yard weeks earlier. Growing up, we played with our siblings and got decent at it.

One by one, the neighbors wandered out. The downstairs guy, a retired federal agent, pulled up a chair. Jerry joined. Raj joined. We drank, played, and listened to stories from lives already lived.

That's when I understood something simple. Out here, in the middle of the Pacific, neighbors matter. Community isn't optional. For a while, life felt unreal in how normal it became. Maui. A great job. Good people. Good rhythm.

Then the island reminded me it wasn't a postcard.

Dalt and I were at Sandbox when a couple of tourists challenged us to beach pong. Halfway through the game, a few cops approached. "Name. Where you stay?" Before I could explain anything, they cuffed me and showed me a grainy photo of a guy they were after. Felony charges. I looked similar, but it wasn't me.

Next thing I knew, I was shirtless and barefoot in a Lahaina holding cell. Cold concrete and the smell of sweat surrounded me. One guy was losing his mind, punching the door until his knuckles split. I sat quietly, watching the shock wash over me.

In that cell, every version of myself merged into one. Paradise wasn't closed off. It had shadows too. By morning, they transferred us to Wailuku. Bigger cell, same confusion. Around lunch that day, they let me go. I wasn't upset. I was just glad to go home.

Jerry and Dalt picked me up. Dalt shook his head and laughed. "You attract the weirdest shit," he said.

That night, lying in bed, I wasn't angry. Just aware. Lying there, my body still hadn't calmed down. Not from fear, but recognition. It felt like the island had been tapping me on the shoulder for months, and now it had my full attention.

Time was moving fast. I'd already been on Maui for eight months. Somewhere in the middle of it, Dalt and I started talking about flying home. Neither of us could really explain why. We weren't unhappy, or stuck. It just came up quietly, like something our bodies knew before we did.

Dalt later said the late-night conversation with the stranger had stuck with him more than he realized. Something about it sat in the back of his mind. Around the island, we had also started hearing people talk about "island fever." It was a real thing. People came and went all the time, days, weeks, months. But if someone made it past two years, they were usually there to stay awhile. Something about that idea lingered with me.

Part of it might have been the simple realization that I had been gone from home a long time, and that nothing lasts forever. So, we bought tickets for a month out.

The ticket felt more like a safety net than a decision. Knowing I had a way home brought a strange sense of calm. Deep down, I think a part of me already knew I wasn't going to take that flight. With time still left, we kept living. Working. Skating late.

One night, Dalt and I joined Jerry at Slaughterhouse Beach. After sunset, we lit a fire. We swam, drank, and met others doing the same. Fires dotted along the shoreline, voices drifting in the dark.

I looked up at the stars, and something familiar settled in. The same feeling I'd had in Bullhead City. I didn't say it aloud, but I recognized it. One more fire. One more cheap beer. Only this time nothing was shooting at me. The fire wasn't outside. It was inside.

The drive home was quiet. About fifteen minutes from the house, coming down the last hill, click. No brakes. Jerry hesitated at the red light. The pedal went dead. The smell hit us immediately, burned metal. He dropped the truck into a lower gear and slowed us just enough to stop before the red light. When the light turned green, we crept home with the hazards on. I remember saying, "If this had happened on one of those corners... we'd be dead."

A few nights before our flight, Michael knocked on the door dressed in a denim trench coat and a golf hat. “We’re going to Haleakala,” he said.

A few hours later, we were ten thousand feet above sea level, freezing, standing above the clouds. The road climbed through mist until the world dropped away beneath us. The volcano looked like Mars, red dirt, lava rock, a silence that didn’t need explanation. I saw my first *nene* glide overhead, calm and rare. The sun sank beneath the clouds in a double sunset, color bleeding across the horizon.

When night took over, the stars appeared. The Milky Way felt close enough to touch. Standing there, above everything, the world didn’t feel overwhelming. It felt exact. I didn’t feel like I was searching for my place in it. I felt like I was already standing in it.

A few days later, we were driving to the airport. Quiet. Internal. When we arrived, we pulled our bags from the trunk and stood there longer than necessary. Standing there with my bag in my hand, I realized something simple. I couldn’t go back to a life that had already decided it didn’t want me. I had spent too long under other people’s stories about who I was supposed to be. I wasn’t interested in defending myself. Out here, I was figuring things out on my own terms. I was conquering fears I didn’t even know I had. Leaving now felt like giving up on that.

Part of me also hoped Dalt would stay. I didn't say it out loud, but I wanted my best friend beside me while we kept chasing whatever this place had in store for us. Bird was already gone, and the idea of being alone again sat heavily in my chest. Still, I knew one thing for sure: getting on that plane meant going back to the chaos I had escaped. Back to the same weight, the same noise, the same version of myself that was slowly destroying his own life. I had left that place because I believed it was where I was going to die. And standing there at the airport, I knew I wasn't going back to it.

I said it.

"I'm not getting on the plane."

For the first time in years, I was choosing my life instead of escaping it. Dalt smiled... He admitted he'd been debating it the entire drive. Jerry watched us, curious, as we went back and forth. In the end, Dalt had already crossed the line. He'd left work, bought the ticket, and said his goodbyes. He was committed.

I wasn't.

Every goodbye felt heavier on the island, and I was going to miss having Dalt there. But I couldn't leave. Not yet. Things were shifting. I wasn't chasing moments. I was paying attention to what they were teaching me.

9

One of those moments came a few days after Dalt left. Michael and Jerry invited me to light the Lahaina Luna High School "L" for graduation. It's a giant L on the top of the mountain above the high school. It can be seen by all of Lahaina. Every year, Alumni hike up and light the L after sunset.

The trail began easily, then turned wild, red dirt, tangled roots, thick brush. Halfway up, heavy rain hit. The mud turned slick. We slipped, slid, laughed, and stained red. You learn quickly why Tide doesn't shoot commercials in Hawaii.

When I broke through the last of the jungle, the world opened up. Lahaina stretched below, islands off in the haze, the West Maui Mountains rising behind us. Then the sun punched through the clouds like a reward.

At the top stood a flagpole and a Hawaiian burial site marked with lava rock and a *lei*. I learned the grave belonged to David Malo. He requested to be buried on Mt Ball, to protect his remains from being disturbed by foreign influence. This wasn't just tradition. It was history. Respect. An honor to be invited into.

The air felt different. Alive. The older alumni lowered the old Hawaiian flag to raise a new one. Then one of them pointed at me. "You, get up there." I didn't know why, but I listened. He handed me the flag. I attached then raised it. The wind snapped the flag clean, and the crowd clapped. Energy rushed through me, like the island itself exhaling.

Standing there, looking out over the lights of Lahaina far below, my thoughts drifted in an unexpected direction. I thought of my daughter. I wondered where she was, if she was okay, if she ever thought about me. I continued reaching out, and still no response.

The feeling didn't hurt the way it used to. It was steady. I wasn't reaching backward. I understood, quietly, that the path to her would be long and difficult, but that a day would come. The thought passed as gently as it arrived.

In that moment, the mask slipped. I felt seen, not judged, not measured. Seen. It didn't feel like praise or approval. It felt quieter than that, like I didn't need to explain who I was to belong there. No one was asking for a version of me that fit better. I was just there, and that was enough.

When darkness came, Alumni lit the "L." Headlights traced the roads below us, the town glowing like something distant but connected. Up there, Lahaina glowed red, the moon bright, the town full of action. Every photo we captured came back with glowing orbs, like the camera caught what words couldn't. I felt small, but exactly where I belonged. That night, the lights of Lahaina stretched below us. I stood there longer than anyone else.

I ended that night with ruined shoes, red stains, a full soul, a smile on my face.

A few days later, Jerry mentioned a surfer pad he'd found on Front Street. Three open rooms, month to month. The kind of place people drift through on the island. Our lease at the house had come to an end. So, we moved.

On the last night in the house, I sat on the lanai drinking a few beers. I stared out into the vast blue, reflecting on the last year. There were memories in that house now.

The sun disappeared, and the water turned dark. I finished the last beer, set the bottle beside me, and sat there a little longer.

10

991 Front Street was unlike any place I had ever called home. When I first saw the house, I recognized it immediately, the same one with the tall mango trees I used to eye from the sidewalk. A small sign on the fence warned, "*Ey No Mango Pickas*!"

The place was the last house before the heart of downtown. Seven bedrooms, two bathrooms, no front door, no back door, and a lifetime of stories buried in its bones. It used to be the Old Lahaina Leisure Club, a real surfer house. Ocean on one side, lava rock sea wall holding back the Pacific on the other. When the tide was high, waves sent mist straight through the living room windows. Sitting on the couch, I was three feet from the water.

Jerry took the first room on the left. I took the first room on the right. Out back was a patio and a couple of steps that led straight into the ocean. Two outdoor showers sat beside them, cold enough to sting, perfect after a swim. Showering at sunset felt holy.

The first thing I did after moving in was pick a basket of mangos. Living there meant the fruit was fair game. That first bite? Onolicious. Juice running down my arms, chest, face. It felt like the island grew those mangos just for me.

Nights were loud with laughter, live music drifting from the bars, tourists spilling down Front Street while the ocean kept slapping the seawall. Being that close to the city felt like plugging into Maui's pulse. The roommates were a wild mix. One guy was climbing Mount Kilimanjaro when I moved in. Another, Spud, worked in restaurants like me. Good dude, solid energy.

Once a week, the house would get together for a movie or show on the projector, the ocean glowing behind it. A *60 Minutes* episode about the founder of Nick Woodman hit me harder than I expected. It wasn't the success that stuck with me. It was the way everything was captured. The angles. The movement. The feeling of being inside it instead of just watching it. I caught myself paying attention to things I normally wouldn't. How a shot was held, how it shifted, what it made you feel without saying anything. I didn't think much of it at the time. But it stayed with me.

In the mornings, I ate breakfast on the patio, watching the waves roll in. Some days I'd swim out to Baby Beach. On others, I'd sit down and write before work.

Music had always been there. That's where *Maui Bound* started. Over a few days, I worked with a friend, DJ Illuminator, building the track piece by piece. When it was finished, I played it for my friends, not knowing what they'd hear in it.

One morning, Michael showed up at the house. “Come to my place,” he said. He had two mics and a small setup ready. He interviewed me about my song. I was nervous, but proud, surrounded by walls stacked with vinyl. Then he brought me to Kihei, cued up my track at the station, and announced it on air. Hearing my song blast through the speakers felt impossible, like the island was showing me a version of myself I never knew could exist. For months afterward, “*Maui Bound*” played across the radio. It was something I would never forget.

Down the street, an outlet mall was reopening after a decade of being closed. I landed a retail job at an athletic shoe store and helped build it from the ground up. On days off, I was back in the water, paddleboard, kayak, whatever floated. I’d cruise along Front Street on the ocean, talk story with tourists, then park my kayak on a tiny downtown beach and watch the sunset. Life felt simple, alive.

What I wasn’t doing was paying attention to money. Rent came due when it was supposed to. Structure still felt foreign. Bills felt like chains. Responsibility felt like losing freedom.

As long as I could work, skate, eat, and stay near the water, I convinced myself I was okay. I avoided looking too far ahead because planning meant admitting how fragile everything actually was. I was choosing comfort over structure.

One night, I actually counted what I had. Not in a bank account, I didn’t even have one. Just cash in my wallet, tips in a jar, loose bills folded in drawers. It wasn't much. If something went wrong, if I lost my job, if rent jumped, if I got hurt, I wouldn't last a month.

I felt it in my chest for a second, a small wave of anxiety. Then I told myself the same story I always did. Everything works out. You've survived worse. Money isn't why you're here. I closed the drawer and went back outside.

One morning, Jerry and another roommate joined me out on the water. We were laughing, catching small waves near the reef, when something massive bumped my board. I looked down and saw a shark, nine feet easy. Thump. The board lifted under my feet. My stomach flipped, but Jerry and the other guy laughed and paddled toward it. That moment taught me; fear is taught long before it's felt. Standing on the water, watching one glide past me while everyone else laughed, I felt the difference between inherited fear and real danger.

A few months after moving in, Jerry finally received the promotion he had been waiting for. A week later, he flew back to the mainland. The house said its goodbyes, and Michael drove him to the airport.

By then, I had been on the island for over a year. Friends and family had come and gone. I had gained experience and begun to change in ways I didn't yet fully understand.

A new roommate moved in, and Halloween came right after. This time, I knew what to expect, and I was ready.

Spud stood in the driveway with a fishing pole and a cardboard hook wrapped in tinfoil.
"Fishing for hotties," he said. It worked.

I drifted through the crowds, moving from bar to bar, costumes blending into each other under the streetlights. At one point, I stopped near the banyan tree, where a costume contest had pulled a crowd tight around the stage. Music echoed through the branches, people shouting, laughing, trying to outdo each other.

It felt like the whole town had shown up.

Later, I met two girls. One from Switzerland, the other from Paris. When the crowd started thinning, we made our way back to my place. We talked for hours, trading stories like we'd known each other longer than we had. They had just spent the summer traveling through Europe. Maui was their last stop before heading home. We skinny dipped, talked about life and death, then ended up under the mango tree. There was no pressure. No expectations. Just a moment. The kind that doesn't ask for anything more than what it is.

The next few days, my focus shifted.

Rent was due. The party was over. I had never been good with money. I didn't grow up around it, never learned how to manage it. I just knew how to make enough to get by, and even that was inconsistent.

This time felt different, though. I was working. I wanted more stability. Something better, for myself, and eventually for my daughter. But I was still learning the hard way. When rent came around, I only had half. I was paying almost double that I had paid living with Jerry, and I hadn't figured out how to keep up with it.

A few days into the month, my landlord asked me to come over. He lived right next door. He was older, calm, observant, the kind of person who didn't speak unless he meant it.

He took the money I had brought, then handed it back. "Tuck this away," he said. I didn't understand. He told me the guys in the house had come together and covered the rest. They didn't want someone new. They wanted me there.

That part stayed with me.

We sat outside for a while, looking out at the ocean. Neither of us said much. Just the sound of the water and the wind moving through the trees.

After a long silence, he finally spoke. "I want you to stay," he said. "But I think you've got more road ahead of you." He said it like it wasn't a question. Like it was already decided.

A couple days later, I was packed. Before I left, I stood in the living room for a while, staring out at the ocean one last time. There was something about that place. Something I couldn't take with me.

I said my goodbyes to the guys, grabbed my things, and headed out. As I stepped through the gate, my landlord stopped me. "Time passes," he said. "You'll always have a place here." I nodded, not really knowing what to say.

Then I left.

Maui had given me more than I knew what to do with. I stepped out of the house with everything I owned in my hands. No plan. Nowhere to go. Just the island in front of me.

That night, I had nowhere to sleep.

PART III
BREAKDOWN

11

The first thing I did was buy a hammock. Then I found three coconut trees on Baby Beach, and tied up a home for myself. My first night was cold and sleepless. No one in the world knew where I was sleeping. Sometime after midnight, I woke up to footsteps in the sand. Close. Too close. I stayed still, listening, trying to slow my breathing. My shoes were out of reach. I remember thinking how quickly things could go wrong and how invisible I actually was. When the footsteps passed, I didn't relax. I stayed awake until morning, because sleep felt more dangerous than fear.

One morning, before my shift, I rinsed off in the outdoor shower and changed into clean clothes I'd washed by hand the night before. I carefully folded my hammock, hid it, and showed up on time. No one there knew where I'd slept, and I didn't tell. I wasn't pretending. I was choosing not to let the worst part of my situation define how I carried myself.

Weeks went by like that.

Cold morning showers to wash the salt from my skin and shake the sand from my shoes, no matter how many times I emptied them.

Some nights, the cops swept the beach.

One night, exhausted and frustrated, I made a bad call. I stayed too close to the water, thinking no one would notice. When the lights hit and the voices started, I froze, unable to move. They didn't arrest me, but they made it clear I'd pushed my luck. Walking away barefoot, heart pounding, I knew I couldn't rely on being overlooked forever. I needed to be smarter, not tougher.

So, I started hanging my hammock twenty feet up, hidden among the trees. It worked. They passed right underneath without noticing. I would be the only one left on the beach when they were done.

Living on the street showed me things I hadn't understood before. I used to see houseless people and wonder where they slept, how they stayed warm, and how they survived. Now I knew. I learned the hidden spots, where to eat, where to shower, and where to charge a phone without being chased off.

Everything boiled down to survival.

The ocean kept rolling in as if nothing had changed.

If people back home saw me sleeping on that beach, they'd probably laugh and say they were right about me. But going back wasn't an option. Somewhere in the world, my daughter was growing up. And some day, she was going to meet the man I was becoming out there.

I'd been hungry, cold, and close to the edge myself. Just like many of the people on the streets. I watched guys stand outside restaurants, asking tourists for leftovers as they carried to-go boxes past him. I knew I would never see the houseless the same way again.

Then came the night everything changed. I woke up knowing I wasn't alone. I'd seen a silhouette on the far edge of the beach earlier, someone standing too still in the dark. Then I heard movement behind me, in the brush where I'd hidden my duffel. I didn't move. I stayed quiet, convinced they hadn't seen me. I stayed awake until the beach went still again.

Morning came, and some of my things were scattered near the trees. My duffel was gone. Walking toward Front Street, I passed the trash bins and saw fabric sticking out. Inside were my clothes, dumped like I didn't matter. Everything with value was gone. Shoes, watches, anything worth money. What stayed behind felt intentional.

I wasn't seen as a person. Just something easy to strip down. It showed me how little margin I'd been living with.

So, I moved. Not because I wanted to, but because staying exposed felt reckless.

I'd climb over the railing, drop down to the sea wall, and hang my hammock between the beams under a local shop. Some nights, high tides splashed me awake. The ocean's breath would hit my face, whispering something I couldn't quite understand. Some nights, it felt like something was rocking me. Other nights, it felt like it wanted to swallow me.

I didn't blame it.

On days off, I walked Front Street from end to end, learning every hidden corner. I lived on coconuts and wild fruit. I even dove for lobster a couple of times. My hands smelled like salt and cracked coconuts.

Despite the exhaustion and cold nights, I felt free. The beach was my front yard. The sky was my ceiling.

I started sand sculpting, couches, sharks, honu, and whales. Tourists loved them. Some tipped me. Some gave gifts. But I didn't do it for that. It was proof I still had something inside me that wasn't broken.

But when the holidays hit, Thanksgiving, then Christmas, the weight returned. The world felt connected, and I was outside it.

One night, after sunset, I headed back to the spot where I slept. When I hopped the seawall, I saw two people going through my duffel.

A man and a woman, both in their forties. The man wore a headlamp, the beam cutting across the sand as he dug through my bag.

I walked over and announced myself. They acted casual, like nothing was happening. Like it wasn't my bag. I told the man to take my watch off. That's when their faces changed. I stood there until they emptied their pockets and returned everything. I let the woman keep a few hygiene items. I'm human, after all.

A few days later, Jerry called. His friend Mike might have a spot in a garage open for me.

On Christmas Eve, uncle Mike called. "Come by," he said. "Get off the beach." I caught the bus with my backpack and skateboard.

The garage he showed me, three walls, a roof, felt like a mansion after months of sand and wind. I didn't feel deserving of help, but I wasn't going to turn it down.

PART IV
INTEGRATION

12

On Christmas Eve, I moved to Honokowai. I thought I understood Maui. I didn't. That little town carried a different kind of gravity, one that would shape me more than anything before it.

The house was tucked just off the main road, deep in a local community. Unlike Lahaina, where tourists and *transplants* mingled without thought, Honokowai felt deeply rooted.

Inside the garage sat a bed, a TV, a few boxes, and warm ocean air. Simple. Raw. Honest.

19

“Howz it?” a voice said behind me. “Aloha, I’m Anthony.” I spoke. “Jerry said you’re a good guy, can stay here while you figure things out.” He spoke.

That was my introduction to uncle Mike. He owned the house, spoke heavy *Pidgin*, and carried himself like a man who’d earned every scar and smile on his face. We talked story for a couple of hours. He didn’t treat me like a guest. He treated me like someone who’d better show respect if he wanted to stay. He lived there with his mother, a quiet woman who only spoke Japanese, and another roommate, Koa, a Hawaiian local who’d known Jerry, Mike, and Michael since childhood.

That first night felt surreal, half discomfort, half peace. I missed the hammock. Sleeping out in the open had changed me. The concrete floor of the garage grounded me in a way I didn’t expect.

Alone, but not alone. Honokowai moved slower. Eventually I did too.

At first things were a cultural dance, with different backgrounds, languages, and habits all under one roof. Sometimes our worlds clashed, but respect always held it together. Slowly, they treated me like one of their own, and I didn’t take that lightly.

Belonging wasn't something I was given here. It was something I had to earn, quietly. And it could be taken just as quietly if I got it wrong.

Living there taught me restraint in ways no adventure ever had. The uncle's moved slowly, deliberately. They didn't explain themselves or posture. Respect came from consistency, not noise. Being around them made me realize how much energy I had wasted trying to prove things no one had asked me to prove. Strength wasn't about how much I could carry. It was knowing when to stay quiet and do what needed to be done.

Communication required effort. Uncle's mother spoke only Japanese. Uncle Koa's pidgin was fast and heavy. Uncle Mike spoke in a rhythm I had to learn. But day by day, I picked it up. I learned more languages in those months than I ever did in school.

Down the street, a small fruit stand sat under a giant almond tree. The smell of ripe mangoes and coconuts hit before you even saw it. A tall, mellow Guyanese man named Deem ran the place. Seven days a week. No complaints. I watched him cut coconuts open with a machete, like he was born to do it. Cameras were always pointed at him. The more I walked by, the more drawn I felt.

Honokowai didn't have the same options as Lahaina, not even close. For the first month, maybe longer, I walked past Deem every morning with the same thought in my chest. I needed a job. But it wasn't just that. I watched him move through the day, steady, unbothered, present. He worked for himself. What he put in seemed to come back directly. His mood didn't rise and fall with customers or money. There was a kind of ownership in him I recognized before I could name it. I kept passing the stand, telling myself not yet, until the wanting stopped feeling optional.

I finally asked if I could help. "You can hang around today," he said. By closing time, I was handling customers, bagging fruit, and cleaning up. Deem watched me with a kind of quiet surprise, then told me to come back the next day. Just like that, I had a job.

The outdoor shopping center where I worked had a tattoo shop, restaurants, moped rentals, and a gift shop owned by Auntie Lu. She liked me right away. Deem lived upstairs in a studio, so between us, the stand never slept.

I wasn't the only new person at the mall.

Most of the businesses were new too, and some arrived after I did. A few studio apartments sat above the shops, and people were always coming and going. Everyone was learning from each other at the same time.

At home and at work, I stayed quiet. Observant. There was too much to learn to pretend I understood any of it.

Something as basic as selling fruit could turn complicated fast when you don't share a language. I stumbled through hand gestures, broken words, and smiles that had to carry more than they should.

So, I became a sponge.

I watched how people moved and how they greeted each other. When they spoke and when they didn't. I paid attention to tone, posture, pauses, and everything that didn't need translation. Slowly, the locals who lived and worked around the mall started noticing I wasn't just passing through. I showed up every day. Same place. Same effort. That mattered more than words.

Uncle Mike and I often shared stories. Long ones. Pieces of our lives were exchanged like we were testing each other's truth. Sometimes he'd shake his head and tell me I'd lived the craziest life he'd ever heard. I thought it was just as wild that he'd lived in the same house his entire life.

One afternoon, he handed me a stack of old shirts that didn't fit him anymore. "You've got to look the part if you're going to sell coconuts island-style," he said. It wasn't about the shirts. It was one of the first times someone here invested in how long I might stay.

That was the gift of that house. Everyone wanted everyone else to succeed, not loudly, not with advice, but by quietly making space for it. Uncle Koa took me surfing at Olowalu. Uncle Mike dragged me to watch football at the bar. They didn't ask me where I was headed next or what my plan was. They treated me like someone who belonged *now*, not later.

If they hadn't opened their home to me, if they hadn't supported my choices without trying to shape them, I never would have had the Honokowai experience. I don't mean the place. I mean the version of myself that learned how to stay.

I planned to stay. Not in a vague, someday way. I chose that life deliberately, and once I chose it, I committed.

Every morning, I'd tell Deem I'd be cutting coconuts in no time, giving him some competition. A friendly *step your game up*. He'd laugh, but he didn't know me yet.

It didn't take long to get comfortable at the stand. Deem and I shared a similar mindset and understood each other quickly, the kind of understanding that doesn't need much explaining. We were good with people, almost unfairly so. Between the two of us, people rarely walked away empty-handed. It wasn't manipulation. It was instinct. We knew how to read people, how to meet them where they were, how to make a moment feel human instead of transactional.

Survival teaches you how to move like that. I recognized it in him right away. I knew he had a story. He didn't offer it, and I didn't ask. Out here, you let consistency do the talking.

After a few months, we started talking about expanding. At first, we kept it simple: mangoes, papayas, coconuts, bananas, dragon fruit, avocados. But the space around us felt unfinished. Too quiet. Too much room left unused.

Honokowai didn't have much compared to Lahaina, just a few local spots, a grocery store, a gas station, and then the resorts. Big hotels on one side, long rows of condos on the other, and small neighborhoods like mine tucked in between.

That contrast mattered.

Uncle Koa would pass the stand on his way to and from work almost every day. Twenty-five years at the same job. Uncle Mike had done the same. I respected the hell out of that. Not because it was glamorous, but because it was steady. That kind of dedication says something about a person. About character. About showing up, whether you feel inspired or not.

At first, Deem was always there when the stand was open. He handled most transactions and business parts himself. Slowly, naturally, a rhythm formed. No formal handoff. No conversation about roles. Just repetition, trust, and time doing what it does best.

The fruit stand wasn't just work anymore. It was a pulse and lifestyle. I stopped getting haircuts. Went barefoot everywhere. Lived off coconut water, coffee, fruit, fish, and sunshine. Life was stripping away everything in me that didn't belong.

Somewhere in the middle of this rhythm, my spiritual side began to wake up. Deem and I were invited to different churches every week, and we said yes to most of them. One Sunday, we ended up at a service in another language. I left my slippahs at the door, sat barefoot, and didn't understand anything except "Aloha" and "*Amen.*" But I felt everything. The warmth, the unity, the reverence, it filled something in me I didn't know was empty.

From then on, Deem and I "*church hopped.*" People joked about it, but I didn't care. Faith wasn't a language to me. It was energy, and Maui was teaching me connection all over again.

Not everyone appreciated how I approached faith. Some said I should pick one church and commit. That asking too many questions meant I didn't believe. The more curious I became, the more uncomfortable some people seemed. It confused me. I wasn't trying to reject faith. I was trying to understand it honestly.

I began to realize that spiritual growth didn't always lead to greater acceptance. Sometimes, it made you harder to identify.

Neither Deem nor I had a car. Sometimes, people offered rides to church, but most mornings started the same way. By the ocean, somewhere quiet. We'd read scripture first, then talk about how to bring the teachings into our day. After we would smoke a spliff. Always in that order. It wasn't a contradiction; it was respect.

To get to church, we hitchhiked. I didn't love it, not out of fear, but self-consciousness. I worried about how it looked, about being seen a certain way. Deem never hesitated. He'd step to the edge of the road, thumb out, calm as if he already knew someone would stop.

Some Sundays, we went nearby. Others, to Lahaina, and sometimes, clear across the island. Between the rides and the services, I met people from all over, people with different backgrounds, languages, and beliefs.

We had a home church in Honokowai, the one we visited most. We opened the fruit stand later on Sundays. Week by week, we kept showing up.

Somewhere along the way, it stopped feeling like something I was trying out.

It became part of my life.

I hadn't grown up with consistency when it came to faith. Church was occasional, mostly around holidays. I always believed there was something more, but it was never something I gave real attention to.

That started to change.

Not all at once. Just small shifts. The way I thought. The way I reacted. The way I carried myself day to day.

Life felt steadier. Less scattered.

I wasn't trying to preach anything or figure out what was right or wrong. I just knew that having something to believe in, something outside of myself, gave me a kind of structure I hadn't had before.

And for the first time in a long time, I wasn't fighting everything.

I wasn't just reading religious texts anymore. I started reading in general. Books like *Nine Faces of Christ*, *The Four Agreements*, and *A Beginner's Guide to Walking the Buddha's Eightfold Path*. Looking back, I hardly read as a kid, maybe just a few required school books. I was to *cool* for reading... This was where it changed. Reading became a way to understand myself and the world around me, to sit with ideas rather than run from them. It slowed me down in a way nothing else had.

Peace was present. But peace is tricky. It often shows up right before life decides you're ready for the next lesson.

13

Those first six months in Honokowai were about establishing roots, home, work, and community.

I started noticing the same guy walking past the stand every day. Barefoot. Quiet. Looked like a surfer, and carried the same look I once did. When he stopped by, he mostly observed. Didn't say much. His name was Varv. Deem and I invited him to hang around and then help with the cleanup at the end of the day. He'd just moved to Maui from the mainland and didn't have much going on yet. The fruit stand fit him. No clock to punch. No script to follow. We paid him, and welcomed him like ohana.

I was rarely home during those days, but when I was, I helped around the house. I ran errands with uncle Mike, sat with his mother as she hummed old Japanese songs, and watched uncle Koa train in jiu-jitsu. Living in the house came with expectations. I was responsible for pulling my weight, inside and outside the home, and it was made clear early on that I had to pay my own way.

As time went on, I wasn't just learning the rhythms of the house. I was getting to know their friends and ohana too. People were always stopping by, staying over, and passing through. When some of them first saw me there, they were confused. Their eyes would light up, trying to place this long-haired, coconut-cutting haole living under that roof. But over time, relationships formed. They saw the help I offered, the respect I carried, and the way I showed up. I went from the quiet new roommate to someone woven into the house's energy. Plus, uncle Mike always had my back.

Once I learned the operations of the fruit stand, I bought in fully. Literally. I invested in *Maui Juice Freeze*. The foundation was solid, even though neither of us really knew what we were doing yet. Deem had only been open for a month or two when I arrived, and we learned everything together. We built a contact list for Maui-grown fruit, earned local regulars, and gradually brought life back into the outdoor mall.

Stank, who owned the tattoo shop, was the first to notice. One afternoon, he took me upstairs and told me something simple but important: we were bringing in twice as many customers as he was used to.

That day, a guy no-showed for a tattoo that Stank had spent hours designing. Instead of letting it go to waste, he offered it to me. A great white shark, swimming through open water. I grabbed a coconut, cracked into it, and went upstairs. It became one of the largest pieces.

I filmed the whole process, before, during, and after. The shop, the energy, the story. When I brought Stank the finished video a few days later, he loved it. He shared it online, and something clicked. A trade system was born. We became the current flowing through that mall.

Meanwhile, the fruit stand was getting busy in a way we couldn't ignore. Deem and I moved in sync, always scheming, always laughing. My machete skills finally caught up to his, and we'd challenge each other with new tricks. We built tables out of surfboards, hung baskets from trees, and turned that little stand into something people talked about.

I wasn't just filming anymore, even if I didn't realize it yet.

That *60 Minutes* episode about GoPro still sat in the back of my mind. Something about it stayed with me.

Whenever I took photos or filmed clips for the fruit stand, I caught myself experimenting, different angles, different movement, different ways of framing ordinary moments. I started paying attention to light, timing, and the feeling a shot carried.

At the time, all I had was an old phone.

But I wanted more.

A GoPro.
A real camera.
Something that could capture what I was starting to see.

So, I started saving money on the side.

Meanwhile, I filmed everything around the fruit stand. Coconut cuts, customers, little moments, random chaos, whatever the day gave me. I posted constantly, always trying new ideas, chasing better shots without really understanding why.

Looking back, that's when it started.

Passion. Passion for film, photography, and storytelling.

At first, I wasn't confident. I was shy, worried about judgment, and uncomfortable stopping people or speaking up. That version of me was gone. Somewhere along the way, I'd punched my way out of my shell. Talking to people became easy, then natural, then something I actively sought.

I started picking up accents quickly. Tone, posture, pauses. Even when I didn't understand the words, I could feel where someone was from. I started using my Japanese when I had the chance. The first time surprised me.

Two women about my age were standing near the stand, talking quietly to each other. I'd been listening without meaning to. They didn't know I understood them. After a few minutes, I looked up and said, in Japanese, *"Welcome to Maui. You're both very beautiful. And yes, the coconuts are cold."*

They froze. Then both turned red at the same time, laughing, shocked that I'd responded at all.

Something I'd once kept hidden was now useful. Alive. I kept working at it after that, practicing with Uncle Mike's mother whenever I could. Slowly, carefully. Respectfully.

People were constantly surprised by how easily I could guess where they were from. It became a quiet challenge I gave myself. Not to label them, but to listen closely enough to notice the details.

And it didn't stop at selling fruit.

People invited me over. Took me out. Shared meals. Talked story late into the night. These weren't transactions anymore. They were exchanges, presence for presence.

I wasn't going to be the quiet guy in the corner again.
That version of me belonged to a different life.
And I wasn't interested in carrying him forward.

I ended up in hundreds of people's vacation photos from all over the world, who stopped for fruit and left with an experience. I started keeping a customer contact book, everyone I met, talked with, or went on an adventure with. They followed me online, shared my work, and kept the stand connected to the stream of people passing through Maui.

Once the stand had been upgraded, we still needed more product. More range. More life.

That's when the day came.

Deem pulled into the lot in an old, beat-up blue car.

We locked eyes as he parked, and we both started laughing.

"What the hell is this for?" I asked.

"Weekly runs to the farmer markets on the other side of the island," he said, grinning.

That was one of the smartest moves I ever saw Deem make.

Not just the car, but what it unlocked.

He popped the trunk and pulled out fruit we'd never carried before. Real local stuff. The kind you don't find unless you show up early and come back often. From then on, we were up before sunrise once or twice a week, crossing the island while it was still quiet. The markets opened just after the sun came up, rows of aunties selling fruit grown in their own yards, mangoes piled in buckets, papayas still warm from the sun.

We didn't rush them. We didn't haggle. We showed up. Again, and again.

Over time, that consistency mattered. Prices softened. Quality improved. Trust formed.

Between those morning runs and the locals who stopped by the stand, we built more variety than anyone around us. We carried fruit that no one else around us did.

Fruit was everywhere, spread across surfboard tables, hanging from the canopy, bundled and stacked wherever there was space.

The stand became a responsibility. It depended on Deem, and they both depended on me.

I had to take days off, carve out time to breathe. That's when I met Sherm.

Down the street was a big resort, sitting beside one of the stronger currents on the west side. The waves weren't always friendly, but I loved that stretch of beach. It was the resort Uncle Koa worked at. I spent time there whenever I could. Sherm was always there, teaching people how to surf. Not just tourists. Locals. Anyone willing to listen. He was a surf instructor from California, steady and calm, the kind of guy who belonged in the water.

I had seen him around. He'd stopped by the fruit stand a few times. Eventually, I asked him what it would take to get on a board. I didn't have one. Sherm bought into the rhythm, just as others had. We sent people his way, and he sent people ours. If there was a board available, I would be in the ocean.

I spent countless sunsets out there, floating between sets while the sky turned orange. It became meditation. Therapy.

The current was strong enough to sweep you out without warning, and Sherm had saved more lives than I could count. I watched him pull people in more than once. I always felt safer when he was around.

To this day, I still send people to him. You can't miss him. He's always on the beach or in the water. Look for the red hat. Tell him I said Aloha.

14

The first year I felt it creeping in again, the pressure that comes from being constantly needed. Honokowai was small. Familiar. Safe. From the outside, it looked like balance. But somewhere in the middle of all that connection, I could feel myself thinning out.

I needed time alone.

Not social alone. Not quiet with people around alone.
Real solitude.

I needed time that belonged only to me. I wasn't burned out. I wasn't unhappy. But I could feel something inside me building pressure, and I'd learned enough by then to know that ignoring it never ended well.

Honokowai had given me stability. The stand had given me momentum. The community had given me grounding. But none of that answered the noise underneath it all. If anything, success made it harder to hear where the noise was coming from.

So, I took a few days off.
Just me and the island.

I'd been running so long that I'd forgotten what standing still felt like. Success didn't quiet the noise inside me; it just drowned it out. Slowing down felt riskier than failing.

I needed space and silence.

During my days off, I experienced the most powerful meditation of my life. At least, that's the simplest way to describe something that cracked me open from the inside. By then, I'd been studying chakras, breathwork, and deep meditation for months. But I wasn't just meditating anymore. I was chasing quiet. Escape. Clarity. Anything that would silence the noise I'd been carrying for years.

Uncle Koa knew a *wahine* who owned a shack in Hana. So, between buses and hitchhiking, I made my way there. The shack was barely larger than a tool shed. The jungle outside was loud with insects and rain. No running water. I shook the dust off the old futon, sat cross-legged, pressed play on a three-hour *OM* chant, and closed my eyes.

At first, it was just sound.
Then breathe. Then a stillness that came from exhaustion.

I hadn't been alone in months.

My thoughts faded. The edges of the room blurred.

And then something shifted. It felt like relief, like slipping out of a too-tight skin I'd been wearing for years.

I saw myself from above, sitting on the futon.
Not dramatic, just distant.
Detached.
Free.

Then I felt a pull, gentle at first, then stronger, a tug from somewhere beyond the walls. I turned toward it and drifted through the shack like the air itself.

Below me, Maui.
Beyond that, the ocean.
Above me, a sky sharp with stars.

Then I was moving, fast, shooting across the Pacific like thought.

I didn't miss the place.
I missed the version of me who never got the chance to grow there.

The pull guided me to an abandoned car wash.
Silent.
Empty.
Middle of the night.

And then she appeared.

A golden-white presence. She looked straight at me, not the me floating above the concrete, but the me I didn't show anyone.

The world froze.

I didn't feel fear.
I felt seen.
Completely.
Quietly.
Without judgment.

For a moment...

Then the pull changed direction, suddenly, strongly, like the universe reminding me I didn't belong there yet. I snapped backward, through clouds and over the ocean.

Cold hit me first.
Then breathe.
Then my heart was pounding in my chest.

I gasped and opened my eyes.

The shack was the same.
But I wasn't.

For days after, I thought about her.
Who she was.
What she meant.

I couldn't explain it.
I didn't try.

All I knew was this:

Whether it happened in the sky or in my own mind didn't matter. Something in me had been spoken to, and it stayed spoken.

When I came back, nothing around me had changed.
The stand still opened in the morning. Fruit still needed cutting. Customers still lined up. Honokowai didn't ask what I'd seen or where I'd gone. It didn't need to.

I didn’t talk about the experience. I didn’t frame it. I didn’t try to make it useful. I just carried it quietly. Whatever had happened didn’t give me answers. It gave me space.

Then life kept moving.

15

Soon after, a local woman stopped by and offered me a job. She hadn't just shown up once. I recognized her. She'd stopped by the stand a few times, made small talk, nothing more. I didn't know who she was or what she did. Her shop was in a resort in Kaanapali. It wasn't just the GoPros. She rented out snorkel gear, waterproof cameras, and accessories.

She was looking to replace an employee who'd been teaching tourists how to use GoPros and operate drones. He was about my age and moving back to the mainland. By the time she made the offer, she'd been watching me for weeks.

I went to see the shop, looked at the system, and talked through expectations. I was excited, but nervous. The kind of nervousness that usually made me back out. This time, I didn't. I said yes.

My first class terrified me. I'd never been comfortable speaking in front of groups. I could feel my face turn red, my hands shake, my words stumble. When it came time for questions, I didn't have answers to all of them. But I kept showing up. Two, sometimes three classes a week. Little by little, the fear loosened.

I had access to the latest cameras, accessories, and drones. I practiced constantly, not just during classes, but also at the fruit stand and out on the water. It didn't just help the shop. It pushed the fruit stand forward, too.

People from the stand came to my classes. People from my classes came to the stand. The momentum fed itself. Our reach grew faster than we could track, spilling into the rest of the mall. For a while, it felt like everything around us was rising together.

I wasn't the only one with another job. Deem had one too, and it lived right there at the fruit stand. We had a small podium with a computer hooked into a company that sold island activities at a discount. Sunset cruises, helicopter tours, luaus, whale watches, and shows. As a rep, Deem got to go on many of them for free. At first, I went along as his plus one. Eventually, I joined the company myself. And of course, I filmed everything. The experiences, the people, the movement. It gave customers something to see, and the marketing fed itself.

The photos and videos started stacking up as fast as life was moving. That's when I started Hempire Studios.

HEMPIRE
studios

At first, it was just a personal media portfolio, something independent, something that belonged to me. I sketched out a rough logo and paid one of Stank's apprentices to turn it into something real. When it was finished, Hempire Studios was official.

From there, things multiplied. When people booked activities through us, I offered to guide, photograph, and film. It became another stream of income and a deeper connection. I also did local work, like creating menus for a Mexican restaurant and a coffee shop. The phone didn't stop ringing, day or night. I'd never felt so immersed in life, busy, too busy growing and learning to look back.

The only time I remember us shutting down was during Hurricane Iselle in 2014. Even though it made landfall on the Big Island, the rain and wind on Maui were unlike anything I'd experienced. It poured for days. Power flickered. Some water supplies were cut off. If I remember right, we stayed closed for five straight days.

You never knew what you'd get when visiting the stand. We constantly had specials from whatever life brought us: Deem landing a giant tuna, me bringing in wild boar. We never let fruit go to waste. If it started to spoil, we made smoothies, juices, purées, or handed it out. If someone came by hungry or thirsty without any money, they didn't leave empty-handed. I'd been hungry on the beach before, and so had Deem.

Getting to know him taught me a lot. Before Maui, he'd lived on the East Coast, caught up in big-city life, addiction, and choices that almost buried him. He joined a church, and they took a trip to Maui. When it was time to fly back to the mainland, Deem stayed. He said God told him to.

Now there we were, two guys who could've disappeared in different ways, running a fruit stand.

Around that time, I ran into Vic. He lived like a wanderer, barefoot, in a hammock, with a backpack, but always had a job and moved with purpose. We caught up on life, and eventually the conversation shifted to money. When I told him I didn't have a bank account or savings, he looked at me like I'd admitted I slept in traffic. Then he pulled out his phone and showed me a few thousand sitting in his account.

That stayed with me all day. It kept buzzing in my head like a mosquito that wouldn't quit. I'd spent years chasing freedom. No one had ever asked if I was building anything with it.

That night, after a shower, I stood in front of the mirror and really looked at myself. I hadn't done that in a long time. Not truly. My hair was wild, and my eyes... that's what stopped me. They weren't dead anymore. They weren't numb. There was fire behind them, experience, and hunger.

But I also saw the truth. I had become rich in many things, but not money. I was spending it just as fast as I made it. Vic didn't just show me numbers. He showed me the next version of myself, one I wanted to grow into.

I opened my first savings account the next day. It wasn't about money. It was about admitting I planned to be here tomorrow.

During that same time, I went back to books. Not just for meaning, but for understanding. Books like *Whatever Happened to Penny Candy*, *Rich Dad Poor Dad*, and *The Art of War*. The more I read, the more I felt a strange mix of excitement and regret. I was learning, but I couldn't shake the feeling that I'd started late. As a kid, I barely read. In my teens, I thought I was too cool for it. Now I understood what I'd missed. That regret is what keeps me reading to this day. If I could spend a lifetime with my nose in books, I would.

Money stopped looking the same to me. I was making real money. But now I tracked it. I built a different relationship with it. That clarity opened doors to investing, expanding, traveling, and upgrading. But it also revealed the leaks. The wasted money. The habits that quietly drained us.

Around that time, something started to stand out to me. The returning customers.

Not just people wandering back through, but people who came looking for us. Whatever experience they'd had the first time mattered enough to pull them back again, and that wasn't something either of us took lightly.

It changed the dynamic.

Deem would take off with people on their second or third visits, and I'd do the same. We weren't selling fruit anymore, we were continuing conversations. Relationships, even if brief. People brought their friends. Told stories about us before we ever met them. We'd become part of their Maui.

That was new for me.

People weren't just passing through my life anymore.

They were coming back.

That meant opening old doors again. When I stopped living as if I were only temporary, the past didn't stay quiet.

16

It was one of those cloudy Maui mornings, misty, quiet, ocean rough and cold. I was sitting on the seawall with a cup of coffee, scrolling through emails, when one stopped me.

A woman I didn't know.
Claiming to be my cousin.
Claiming she knew my father.

My breath caught, not dramatically, just enough to let me know something old and buried had woken up. I'd never met my biological father. Not once. I'd only seen a single photo when I was thirteen, a blurry snapshot of someone I wasn't sure I even wanted to understand.

When I was young, I observed other fathers. I noticed how they stood close to their kids in public and lowered their voices when talking to them. I remember waiting after school and watching dads arrive for games, practices, and school events. I always wanted that. I just felt a sense of emptiness I didn't yet have words for.

We exchanged a few messages. Her tone was heavy, careful. After work, I called her.

"My dad and your dad are brothers," she said, voice trembling.

We talked for a bit. Then she said, "Hold on... he's right here."

A pause.
Then a voice:

"Hello?"

It was deep. Calm. Older.
And it sounded like mine.

"I've been looking for you a long time," he said.

I froze.
Hearing him felt like hearing the ghost of a man I might've become if life had twisted differently. His voice carried gravel, weariness, and a strange familiarity that hit me in the chest.

We talked story for three hours.

Part of me was angry that he got to show up now, with nothing left to give, after missing the years when it actually mattered.

He told me about his life, in and out of prison, unhoused, battling cancer.

Later, my cousin sent me a photo.
He looked older than his age, worn thin, tired around the eyes.
I didn't know what to feel.

That night, I called my mother.
"Go at your own pace," she said.
"Stay true to yourself."

A week later, I talked to him again.
The cancer had come back. This time, it wasn't leaving.

He sent me a newspaper clipping, him gardening outside a care home, smiling in the way people smile when they've accepted something the rest of us avoid.

Then he died.

I just kept moving, because if I stopped, the truth might stick. But that night, barefoot in the sand at Honokowai Beach Park, it caught up.

The grief wasn't what I expected.
I wasn't heartbroken or angry.
I was... disappointed.

Not in him, in the space between us. In the years wasted. In the versions of him and me that never got to meet. How do you mourn someone you've never met? How do you feel pain for someone who shares your blood but not your memories?

I wasn't sad about losing a father.
I was sad for the kid I used to be.

Waiting shaped me more than his absence. Losing him showed me exactly what I refused to become.

What scared me was how easily I recognized parts of myself in his story, and how thin the line felt between his life and the one I could still choose.

So, I made myself a promise that night on the sand:
I would be the man who stayed, not the man who vanished, the man who ran, or the man who left damage in his wake. I would break the cycle.

The ocean whispered that night, the same voice I'd heard before. Calm. Steady. Patient. In that dark, salt-soaked moment, I felt something.

Peace.
And fire.

17

For days after my dad died, the idea of what he left behind sat heavy in my chest.

Not emotionally. Financially.

There wasn't much.

I knew what it felt like to live without. I had watched stability disappear overnight more than once. Seeing how little remained after a lifetime made something in me tighten.

I wasn't going to let that happen on my watch.

I started putting money away, no matter how tight things felt. Small amounts. Random amounts. Consistent amounts. It didn't matter how slow it grew. What mattered was that it existed.

If I didn't change, I would be broke forever. I wasn't going to drift into old age and leave nothing behind but stories.

I wanted the next version of me somewhere out in the world to have a better starting point than I did. More opportunity. More support. More proof that someone had been thinking ahead.

My dad's death changed that in me.

I wasn't going to die broke.

Over that year and a half at the stand, rituals formed. One of them was pool hopping along Kaanapali Beach. Eventually, security would catch on and move us along, so we'd head to the next one, working our way down the coast until we ended up at Whalers Village.

Most days felt like that, sunburned, salt-soaked, and moving too fast to notice how quickly time was slipping by.

Back at the house, life stayed busy in quieter ways. One afternoon, I was invited upcountry to watch Uncle Koa receive his purple belt in jiu-jitsu. When I first met him, he was a white belt with a couple of stripes. Over time, I watched him show up to training day after day, tired, sore, older than most of the guys on the mat, never making excuses.

He was pushing fifty.

I had been carrying this quiet weight that time had already slipped away from me. The wasted years. The drifting. The energy spent running instead of building. Somewhere deep down, I felt late to my own life.

But rain or shine, tired or not, Uncle Koa showed up.

Some nights he'd come home exhausted, sit on the porch in silence, and let the breeze dry the sweat before even stepping inside. He told me more than once, "I just ready for give up boo." But the next day, he went back anyway.

I watched the work behind the scenes. The soreness. The repetition. The discipline. And then I watched the moments it paid off.

Standing there while he received that belt stayed with me in a way I didn't expect. The pride on his face wasn't loud or dramatic. It was quiet and earned. Real.

He was living proof that it wasn't too late to become who you were willing to work for.

Time slips for all of us. I had spent years feeling like it was already gone. Watching him made me realize I still had time left to ride the wave. Sometimes that wave wiped me out. But I always got back up.

Uncle Koa helped me understand that my clock hadn't run out yet.

Life was good, and I was riding the waves. One afternoon, sitting alone in my room, coconuts scattered around me, some cracked open, some still full, I noticed something simple and undeniable. I was healthier than I'd ever been. Physically. Mentally. I had stopped fighting who I was.

I'd also come to terms with something I'd avoided admitting for a long time. A nine-to-five job, working for someone else, was never going to fit me. I was built to create, to build, to work for myself. That path wasn't easier, but it was honest. And I was okay with that.

With everything moving so fast, I decided to step away from the teaching job. I didn't just leave. I talked with her, told her how grateful I was for the opportunity, and stayed on until she found a replacement. On my last day, she handed me a gift basket. Inside were a drone, cameras, and accessories.

There was a handwritten card tucked in with them: *One missed class. Mahalo.*

I never told her why I'd missed it.

The truth was simple and a little ridiculous. The night before, I'd gone out for drinks with a woman I'd met from Argentina. Two young people, a beach, a night, it got wild. Somewhere in the chaos, I took a knee to the eye. I didn't realize how bad it was until the morning. Black and blue. A real shiner. I called out with a weak excuse and spent the day with Deem instead, filming a coffee farm fundraiser for the Maui Food Bank.

She was there that day too, supporting the event with a friend. We talked briefly. She definitely saw my eye. We never mentioned it.

That felt right. Some moments don't need explaining. Gratitude mattered more than confession.

I liked being busy, but before I cut things down, my schedule was chaos. The stand was the heart of everything. As long as it was healthy, everything else worked.

It made me start thinking about what came next. Not because I was bored, but because things had begun to repeat themselves. The same locations. The same shots. Different faces, same frames. I didn't want to burn out. I wanted to grow.

So, I slowed down. I turned down work. For a while, I focused less on gigs and more on the art itself, learning to see again and filming what naturally pulled at me through my own eyes.

I wanted to film a short docuseries. About hitchhiking and the lives of hitchhikers. Not the romantic version. The real one. The people between places. The reasons they moved. The risks they carried. The quiet rules they lived by.

The idea stuck with me.

A year earlier, I might have dismissed it. Hitchhiking used to feel reckless, desperate, something you did when you had no other options. But Maui had changed how I saw it. Hitchhiking to church, Lahaina, or home from a beach, I woke up jagged on. I'd lived it long enough to understand the difference between danger and trust, between movement and escape.

Perspective and perception were things Maui kept giving me, whether I asked for them or not.

I started filming quietly. No schedule. No pressure to publish. Just collecting moments. Listening. Letting people talk themselves into being known. I edited when it felt right and stored the rest away. This wasn't content; it was observation. Another way of learning how people move through the world when nothing is guaranteed, and everything depends on the next decision.

In a strange way, it mirrored where I'd been, and where I was no longer willing to return.

I was high on the Maui lifestyle, the attention, the parties, the late nights, the adrenaline. I was living fast on joy, confidence, and connection.

I always crossed paths with other creators, people building brands, chasing ideas, finding their own momentum. Collaboration became second nature. We shared posts, swapped energy, and amplified each other. My reach stretched far beyond the island.

One of those collaborations brought me back to something older. Stank invited me to help with a skateboarding competition in Lahaina, held at the local skatepark. A shop was closing down, and skaters of every age showed up. I filmed the whole thing, took photos, and helped promote the local businesses. Standing there, camera in hand, watching kids and grown men take turns dropping in, I thought of something.

Skateboarding had been part of my life long before Maui. I first got a board at fourteen, just trying to keep up with a friend who was already skilled. I skateboarded every day and dreamed about it at night. When a small shop opened back home, the only one nearby, I entered a competition, feeling I had something to prove. Minutes before my run, a guy on a bike clipped me. I went out cold. I woke up bloody, concussed, stitched up inside and out.

I never quit skateboarding.

Remembering that while standing in Lahaina mattered. It reminded me that before the attention, before the momentum, before the noise, I'd always had something that kept me moving forward.

Not every day can be good.

I went home for lunch to find everyone gathered in the garage. No one said anything at first. I felt it before I understood it, the air heavier, the kind of quiet that warns you not to rush. Uncle's mother was dying. She'd been fighting for a long time, and Uncle had been caring for her quietly, the way he did everything.

We took turns going into her room.

When it was my turn, I sat beside her and held her hand. I said a few things in Japanese. Tried to make her smile. Tried to give something back, even if it was small. She squeezed my hand once. Not long after, she passed. Peacefully.

I stayed at the house for a while, then went back to work. There wasn't anything else to do. Grief doesn't always ask for ceremony.

The house felt different after that.

She had been one of the last things uncle Mike had left, and we could all see the weight of it settle onto him. No one filled the space. No one tried to fix it. Silence moved in and stayed.

The real kind.
The honorable kind.

My father had left nothing behind but a story. Watching Uncle lose the last person who knew his reminded me how quickly even those disappear.

Even now, when it rains, I still hear her singing Japanese songs.

That silence followed me.

It made me think of the people I'd left on the other side of the ocean. Family. Loved ones. Voices I knew by heart but hadn't heard in too long. I'd been distant without calling it that, missing calls, leaving texts unanswered, telling myself I'd get back to them when things slowed down.

Watching the house absorb that loss reminded me how quietly the clock moves.
And how suddenly it stops.

You don't always get warnings. You don't always get one last conversation that ties things up neatly.

I didn't rush to fix anything or make promises I couldn't keep. I just held the thought close that presence matters more than timing, and regret is usually built out of conversations that never happen.

So, I kept it in the back of my mind.

Maybe it was time to reach out, before silence decided for me.

18

Those days, I started getting jag more often. I was rarely without a spliff, and Deem always had champagne close by. It was indulgence dressed up as celebration.

Who could blame us? We were two healthy young men. Who made good money, chased ideas, handed out experiences, and lived inside something we'd built with our own hands.

It was like a show, loud, attractive, always on.
Between tourists and friends, the party never really stopped. Days blurred. Seasons slipped by without announcement.

That's when I began noticing things I hadn't before.

At first, the surrounding businesses were grateful. We brought energy. Foot traffic. Money. But when the slow seasons hit, when tourism dipped, and the island tightened, the mood shifted. That's when the stares got longer. Conversations sharpened. Tension crept in where there hadn't been any.

The mall felt the slowdown, but the stand stayed steady.

And that steadiness changed how people looked at us.

It became clear who celebrated us for what we built and who liked us only when that success spilled over onto them. That wasn't my responsibility, but I had to remind myself of that more than once.

We weren't greedy. We took care of our own. No matter the season, we supported what surrounded us.

But that period taught me something I hadn't understood before.

Real greed doesn't always announce itself.
Sometimes it watches quietly and waits.

As Deem and I approached two years at the fruit stand, I felt the air begin to change, and the distance between where we'd started and where we were felt unreal. But the landlord wanted more as we made more. Vendors saw our success and raised prices. They said things like, "You can afford it." Conversations carried an edge they hadn't before. Our little corner suddenly looked valuable to people who hadn't noticed it when it was quiet.

Jerry came back to Maui and needed a place to land. The house was full, but auntie lu had a studio open next to Deem, so Jerry moved in. I remember those first few days, watching him walk from his place straight to the stand, lingering nearby, trying different things, observing Deem and me in motion.

Eventually, he said it out loud. He couldn't believe how far we'd taken it. How much we'd leveled up. Hearing it from someone who knew me before any of this made the change feel real and heavier than I expected.

A few weeks after Jerry moved back, we overheard a conversation that quietly changed everything.

Deem called me over, calm but urgent. When I stepped into his studio, Jerry was already there. They were sitting near the vent that connected to the unit below.

I'd never been the eavesdropping type. This wasn't curiosity. This was proximity.

The landlord was talking about the fruit stand.

Not casually. Not hypothetically. She spoke about it as if it were already decided, how much potential it had, how it could be run, and who she'd bring in. Family. Friends. People she trusted. People who weren't us.

It landed slowly.

She owned the mall. She owned the space. And now she wanted what we'd built inside it.

I didn't feel rage. I felt something colder. A mix of betrayal and clarity. Offended, yes. But also, aware. There was a strange gratitude in it too, the kind you only feel when the universe pulls a curtain back before things turn ugly.

We didn't confront her.
We didn't tell anyone what we'd heard.

The three of us just sat with it.

Sometimes, the moment that changes your life doesn't come with shouting or confrontation. Sometimes it arrives quietly, through a wall, in a voice you weren't meant to hear, letting you know that the ground you're standing on isn't as solid as you thought.

And once you hear something like that, you can't unhear it.

The week that followed was quiet.

Not outwardly, business moved as usual, but between Deem and I, something unspoken settled in. We didn't talk about what we'd heard. We didn't need to. Somewhere inside both of us, the idea had already taken root. Our days at the fruit stand were numbered.

I showed up the same way I always had. Full spirit. Open hands. Honest work. If anything, I gave more of myself than before, longer conversations, deeper attention, the most genuine experiences I could offer. Not out of desperation. Out of respect.

I knew the morning would come when I'd wake up, and the wall we'd built everything against would be gone. I didn't know the exact day. I didn't rush it. I just worked as if every interaction might be the last one that mattered.

Some endings don't announce themselves.

They let you finish what you started.

Then the night came.

It was three in the morning when I woke to yelling. The voice instantly registered with me. Deem. I ran barefoot through the night in nothing but *bebadeeze*. By the time I reached the stand, cops had him pinned against the car. He was shouting scripture, crying out to God. Not frantic. Raw. Something breaking open.

People whispered around us.

I saw pain.

They finally calmed him down, loaded him into another car, and drove off. I stood there, adrenaline shaking through me.

The next morning, people asked what had happened. I had no answer. Later, Deem called. He said it was a religious experience. I didn't argue. But I knew the truth neither of us said out loud. Something had cracked. The wind was about to change direction. We never spoke about that night again. But I felt it.

The incident with Deem gave auntie Lu a reason.

She had the right. A few wrong moves stacked quietly on top of each other until they were tall enough to point at.

She didn't raise her voice. She didn't explain herself.

She didn't need to.

Deem was told he had until the end of the month.

No argument would've changed it. No appeal worth making. What had been overheard weeks earlier had already set the direction. This just made it official.

Watching it happen, I didn't feel surprised. I felt confirmed. The shape of the ending finally showed itself. Not dramatic. Just final.

We packed without ceremony. No speeches. Just the sound of things being lifted, moved, erased from a space that had once felt permanent. The stand still opened every morning. Fruit still needed cutting. Customers still smiled as nothing had shifted.

But the center was gone.

And when the center goes, everything else becomes temporary again.

That was when I understood that building something doesn't guarantee you get to keep it. Sometimes it just proves you were capable of it.

Maui had shaped me.
Then it tested me.

Now it was doing what it had always done best, clear space.

Deem tried hard to convince me to stay and run it. Something in me said *don't*. Auntie Lu understood. She knew Deem belonged there, that the stand was part of his path. She was right. And I could feel that change was already in motion for me.

The questions came quietly at first. What would life look like without the fruit stand? Would I lose momentum? Had I grown, or was Maui just holding me?

I stopped sleeping.
Night after night, I lay awake, exhausted, my mind running circles in the dark.

Maui has a way of letting you know when a chapter is done.

I thought about my daughter. I wanted to know she existed somewhere in the world, moving forward in time. If she looked like me.

I didn't know.

I booked a flight back to the mainland. Not permanently. Just long enough to face the old versions of myself.

It felt wrong to leave the place where I was transforming. But staying felt dishonest. I wanted to know the change was real.

In the days before leaving, I moved slowly, as if I were trying to memorize the island. The light. The colors. The quiet.

Three days before my flight, Deem and I opened the fruit stand for the last time.

By then, we'd told most of our regulars. Word traveled fast. We were busy all day. Locals, returning visitors, friends who'd become part of the rhythm, all showed up. We sold out before sunset. I caught myself repeating the same thought over and over: *I'm really going to miss this.*

Late that night, we closed the stand permanently.

We didn't do it alone. A small group of friends stayed to help us pack everything down. Nothing fancy, just hands moving quietly in the dark. When the work was finished, we stood together under the canopy one last time and prayed as a group. Then we lingered, talking story the way we always had, letting the moment stretch until it naturally let us go.

Deem moved in down the street, and I gathered my things at uncle Mike's house and started preparing to leave.

I was not leaving empty handed. I had helped build, operate, and lose a business. I had learned life lessons. I had ohana, friends, and passions. Most of all. I knew who I was.

The island kept moving, even as I stepped away from it.

The night before the flight, I slept on the beach.

I talked to Maui the way people speak to God when they're unsure and humbled. I thanked her for everything she'd given me, and everything she'd burned out of me. I asked her to bring me back safely.

"If I'm gone too long, pull me home," I said.

19

When I landed on the mainland, Dalt picked me up from the airport. The shift was immediate. Cars flying by at eighty. The sky dull. Everything rushed and loud.

Before anything else, I went straight to his grave.

I didn't ask for signs. I just stood there, breathing, letting the weight settle. For the first time in a long time, the visit was good. Necessary. Like checking a compass before walking into unfamiliar terrain. I thought of his mother, if she found peace as I did.

The first few days were hazy, like static over everything. Everyone wanted to see me, go out, and talk story.

But that wasn't what I came back for.

I knew I'd only be around for a month or two, so I picked up shifts at Sanford's. It had always been one of the coolest restaurants in the area, with more beer on tap than anywhere in town. Strangely, it felt like my Maui away from Maui. Familiar faces. Controlled chaos. A world I already knew how to step back into.

Dalt worked there. Bird did too. We'd all worked there for years before and after our travels. The kind of place where you could disappear for a while and still be welcomed back as if nothing had changed.

I focused on work first. The routine helped. Shifts blurred into late nights and loud laughter, the kind that fills space quickly and leaves just as fast. Between shifts, I started visiting friends and family one by one instead of all at once.

My auntie had just beaten cancer. So, we celebrated another chance at life. She had always felt like a second mother to me, not just an auntie. Being there for that mattered.

People kept telling me I looked different. Calmer. More patient. I didn't hear it as praise. It felt more like a reflection, something easier to notice here than it had been on Maui.

And that difference followed me everywhere.

There were people I didn't reach out to.

Old friends, I used to get in trouble with. People who had taken advantage of my kindness. Everyone seemed to expect the old Anthony, the one who wouldn't say no. Facing them again made the distance obvious, even when nothing was said out loud.

They weren't reacting to anything dramatic. They were reacting to absence. To boundaries that hadn't existed before. To a tone in my voice that didn't ask for approval.

The fear that used to follow me in crowded rooms had gone quiet. In its place was something simpler. The only fear I carried was of not living. I felt the weight of my own choices in a way that didn't feel heavy. It felt earned.

But something still felt unfinished.
Something waiting on the other side of the ocean.

I could feel it calling me back. Not softly. Not sweetly. A pull in my gut. A whisper in my instincts. The knowing that comes from the bones, not the brain.

Go home.

I got on the plane with clarity and the understanding that whatever I was becoming would have to survive the real world, or it wasn't real at all.

When I was on the mainland?

I was unanchored.

But I understood something important. It was always about consciousness and mindset.

I went back to the island. But even with my feet on Maui again, the question lingered. What would I do now? I didn't know everything yet. All I knew was I wasn't finished. Maui wasn't finished with me.

20

I stopped by the old house first. Said aloha. Jerry was still there. The uncles were happy to see me. A few new faces had filled the empty rooms, and the house felt full in a way that made it clear my time in that space had passed. No conversation about it. Just the quiet understanding that life had kept moving while I was gone.

I grabbed coffee at Java Jazz, the same place that had once felt like routine. On my way out, I ran into Varv, and we talked story for a bit. When I mentioned I didn't have a place yet, he told me to follow him.

He was staying with a friend he'd come to the island with. She had a small studio just around the corner from Uncle Mike's. Varv asked me to wait outside for a few minutes. When the door opened again, he told me I could stay for a month or two. There was a futon. That was all I needed.

Most nights, I slept out on the lanai.

Deem was living just a few blocks away. And somehow, even though I was back in the same neighborhood, everything felt slightly out of place. Losing it felt like a piece of me had disappeared with it.

That stand taught me discipline and confidence. It was the first time in my life I felt rooted, and roots were new to me.

And beneath the surface, under all the logic and the "it's time," there was a fear I kept trying to ignore. What if I never build anything like that again? What if I already hit my peak and didn't even know it?

That scared me more than losing the stand itself.

Because the fruit stand wasn't a success, it was *proof* that I could become someone better. I questioned if that version of me was temporary, and that fear pushed me to wander. To walk the beaches at night. To stare at the ocean and try to hear answers that weren't coming.

And yeah, I distracted myself. Star wasn't love. She was intensity. She was chaos wrapped in beauty. It wasn't romance. It was anesthesia. She understood that, and so did I.

The first time I saw her, we didn't meet. It was late, one of those nights when Honokowai felt empty, and the town went silent early. I'd gone out skating and ended up at the beach park, sitting for a while before heading home. The streets were empty when I started skating down the middle of the road.

Then I heard another board.

At first, just the sound. Wheels against pavement somewhere in the distance. I stepped off my board and started walking, trying to figure out where it was coming from. A shape moved along the sidewalk ahead of me. As I crossed toward my building, she turned into the same entrance.

I was a few steps behind her when we reached the doors. We made eye contact for a second. She smiled, then disappeared into the unit next to mine.

I didn't know many women who skateboarded. I remember thinking it was badass.

A few days later, I passed her and her friends, and she threw me a shaka. Still no introduction. That came later, through Jerry. He was working on Front Street in Lahaina, and Star worked with him. He told her he had a friend she should meet. He told me the same thing about her.

The night we actually met, I was in Lahaina with Deem. He headed off on an adventure, and I caught a ride home with Jerry after his shift. Star was catching a ride, too. Jerry made the introduction, then dropped us off back in Honokowai.

We talked story for a while after that. Started skating together. Sunset cruises. Skateboarding through quiet streets at night.

That's how it began.

Deem started working in Lahaina for the company tied to the computer we'd used at the fruit stand. Vic helped me land a serving job at a golf course just down the road. Life settled into a quieter rhythm.

Honokowai became my place of peace. The town went quiet early, the kind of quiet that could make you feel like you were the only person left awake on earth. The sky felt wider there.

Clearer. I spent most nights alone, skating or walking, letting the ocean fill the silence. When I wanted noise or movement, I'd head into Lahaina.

During those months, I learned one of the most important lessons of my life.

Deem noticed it first. One day, he mentioned that auntie Lu had started trying to bring the fruit stand back. I had to see it for myself. When I finally went by, it was simple. Familiar in shape, but missing something I couldn't name yet. An attempt to follow what we had built.

At first, I won't pretend I handled it perfectly. There was jealousy. Some anger. A tightness in my chest I didn't want to admit to. Watching something you helped build continue without you is a strange kind of grief.

But I kept watching.

Different attempts came and went. Nothing stuck. People didn't gather the same way. The energy never settled in. The stand existed, but the life inside it never returned.

That's when it finally clicked.

It had never been about the fruit.

It had been about the people. The conversations. The relationships. The experiences Deem and I created every day. What we built wasn't a stand. It was an atmosphere people wanted to be part of.

And that realization changed everything.

Wherever I went, whatever I built next, it wouldn't depend on a location. It would depend on me.

Letting go became easier after that. Gratitude replaced the weight. I felt ready to move forward.

Deem started talking about moving closer to Front Street. The daily drive was wearing on him, and the pull of Lahaina hadn't faded. The flow of people. The energy. The opportunity.

He found a small studio right in the heart of town. It wasn't perfect, but it made sense. We could split the rent.

We had a couple of weeks before the place would be ready. I tied up what I needed to in Honokowai and prepared to move again.

Lahaina felt familiar. I missed it.

Before the move, Jerry and a group of friends invited me to camp out on the Hana side of the island. I had always loved that part of Maui. Quiet, wild, untouched. If I could live anywhere long-term, it would be there. I used to say that I'd retire there one day.

I invited Star, and we joined the group.

That side of the island feels different. Rougher. Wilder.

Everyone pitched tents. I strung my hammock between two trees and built a raised bed under it with bamboo and banana leaves. Star thought I was crazy, but she was all in.

It rained part of the night, and waves crept closer than I expected. I was glad I'd built the bed off the ground.

For a few days, we chased waterfalls, swam, and let time stretch the way it only can out there.

A few days later, it was time to move. I got a ride into Lahaina late one night. Deem had already been there for a few days. The complex was concrete and gated, three stories of small studios stacked together. Ours was on the top floor, with a large window facing the West Maui Mountains.

Right in the heart of Front Street. The pulse.

Neighbors watched us move in the way people always do in tight spaces, curious, observant, measuring new energy against old routines. I found myself doing the same thing back, watching, listening, trying to understand the place.

Lahaina felt familiar. It was where everything had started for me. The beginning. The struggle. The months of being houseless. The version of my life that forced me to grow faster than I expected.

I thought I knew this place. Maybe too well.

What I couldn't see yet was the version of myself that was about to arrive there. The one I hadn't met yet. The one I wouldn't have recognized if someone had tried to describe him to me.

Some chapters don't open loudly. They begin while you're still unpacking.

21

It didn't take long for me to adjust to the studio. Losing the fruit stand had sharpened something in me. I was quieter. More observant. Less interested in proving anything.

Understanding that the fruit stand had been about me, not the location, completely changed my mindset. The ideas never stopped. I was still filming everything, and still paying attention to the stories moving around me.

The first few months in the studio were surprisingly quiet. Aside from Varv, not many people had been over. Even though life outside was speeding up, I took time to settle in, learning how to share a small space, building routines inside and outside, and figuring out that new chapter.

Getting to know the neighbors happened naturally. Just outside C Block was a small courtyard surrounded by tall privacy fences and locked gates. A picnic table, a grill, a patch of grass. Nothing fancy, but it became a gathering place. No matter the time of day, someone was usually out there doing something. You never knew what you were going to walk into.

One guy was a retired professional soccer player from Brazil. Some nights we'd sit outside smoking spliffs, trading stories, and talking about what a happy life actually looked like. Corky lived below us, a comedian constantly performing live shows and chasing her dream without hesitation. Around the corner lived Boogie, a legend I didn't yet know would become a close friend. C Block felt like a vertical version of my old house, a strange, perfect mix of people thrown together by the island, a melting pot stacked three stories high.

For the most part, all of us got along.

Work, though, was a question mark. I hadn't lived a "normal" job in two years. Stepping back into it felt strange at first, like trying on clothes that didn't quite fit yet.

I went all in on the sales company behind the activities that had once flowed through the fruit stand. The same system. Just a different stage.

There were about ten of us working the booths on Front Street. Most of them had seen our names in the system for years but had never attached faces to them.

Now they could.

Three of the booths were visible from our studio window, less than a minute's walk away. Watching them from above felt oddly familiar. Freedom to walk away and get lunch or talk to people. The same mix of hustle and connection that had fueled the stand.

The difference was the scale. Compared to Honokowai, Front Street never slept. And I was right in the middle of it.

I went back to the books, sales, psychology, and anything that sparked curiosity. One of my favorites at the time was *Big Trouble* by Dave Barry. It didn't teach me how to sell, but it reminded me not to take life too seriously, which turned out to be just as useful.

The first few months were rough financially. I was better with money now, but income wasn't consistent yet. Some paychecks were thousands of dollars. Some were nothing. Zero. That took time to accept.

Working the booths had its perks, though. We carried free appetizer and dessert cards with our names on them. Every month, the restaurants would tally them and load our gift cards. I started visiting every hotspot on Front Street without spending much at all. Activities were free. Adventures were currency. And whenever I connected visitors to other experiences, I got a cut.

At work, I was getting to know the other activity specialists. Conversations drifted between investments, closing sales, and finding new ways to lead the industry. I wasn't the only one living a chaotic schedule. There were plenty of people who seemed never to sleep, yet somehow always found a way to make money.

One night, after a long day of work, I rolled a spliff and grabbed my skateboard. Something about cruising Front Street in the middle of the night, when everything was quiet, always cracked something open in me. It felt like slipping into a secret version of Maui that only the restless ever saw.

When I passed Lahaina Luna Road, I stopped. Memories of bombing that hill with Dalt hit me like a movie reel, him laughing, me yelling, both of us flying. Without overthinking, I walked up the hill. Halfway up, I sparked my spliff. When I reached the top, I sat on my board, staring out at Lahaina and the ocean. The moon was bright, casting shadows across the water, and the wind felt older than everything I'd survived.

I was just... there.

In that stillness, something hit me.

I wasn't the young man who drank himself numb, who dug through the snow searching for his son's gravestone. I wasn't the kid who wanted to disappear from the world. That night, I felt like I could finally reach back in time and wrap my arms around my younger self. Tell him he wasn't alone. He didn't have everything he needed, but I do now. And I was there for him in a way no one had ever been there for me.

I hopped up, dropped onto my board, and pushed off. For a moment, I pretended Dalt was next to me again. I held my spliff in one hand and carved down the hill, letting the wind slap the past off me. I skated through the blinking lights, across the highway, and down to Front Street as nothing in the world could touch me.

I walked around for a bit, letting memory guide my feet. I stopped by the spot where I used to hide my hammock under the shop. I passed the beach I used to kayak to, the places I'd worked, the sidewalks I'd bled and built on. I lay down on the bench where I used to watch the sunset when I was houseless.

Staring up at the sky, my inner voice whispered, “It’s okay. Let it go, Ant.” And I finally did. The rush hit hard, not sadness, not grief, not guilt. It was release. A weight I’d been dragging for years just... slipped off.

I never cried the morning my son died.
Not at the funeral. Not after.
Back then, I called that strength.
It wasn’t strength. It was survival.

I was proud of who I was becoming.

On the skate back, I started thinking about work. About the chaos. About the next chapter. I wanted more free time, not for rest, but because I had a new fear unlocked.

Not the fear of dying.
Not the fear of failing.

The fear of not experiencing enough. Life suddenly felt too short for anything slow.

So, I picked up serving and bartending shifts on Front Street. More structure, more hours, more connections. Deem sent people to me, and I sent people to him. We fed each other’s hustle like some underground ecosystem of favors, secrets, and hookups.

I stayed with the activity company, working once a month. I wanted to keep the perks.

Every day felt like a movie. Wake up. “Lights, camera, action.” Board, coffee, surf, work, link up, sunset, repeat.

Spam musubi for breakfast, “cheehoo!” at the boys, ocean by morning, work by noon, adventure by night. I had settled in. Front Street was home now, loud and alive and full of opportunity.

BLC

Around that time, Rory started showing up more and more. Deem and I had both seen him working on Front Street before, and he'd worked for the same company at one point. It didn't take long before you could find the three of us together almost daily, crossing paths between booths, grabbing food, and talking story between sales.

Rory was in sales, too, but his situation was different. He was the only Caucasian working for the Israeli business owners on Front Street. Most of the guys around him were deep into the luxury lifestyle, nice cars, designer clothes, expensive cologne trailing behind them. Rory was still entry-level, not quite in that world yet, watching it from the edge while figuring out how to climb into it.

Somewhere in that space, the three of us clicked. Same hustle. Same late nights. Same belief that we were building toward something bigger than where we stood.

Before long, it felt like we moved as a unit.

C Block became our tribe. Some nights, the doors were open, and music flowed from one studio to the next. On other nights, the whole complex went silent. That silence didn't feel empty. It felt like the moment before lightning hits. A warning and a blessing. It told me something was coming. Not a bad storm. A beautiful one. I was free to go full speed. And I was ready.

One night on Front Street, I ran into Star.

We cruised the strip for a while, talking without effort, the kind of conversation that doesn't ask where it's going. I recognized that energy immediately.

Back at the studio, the windows were open, and the street noise drifted in through the dark. There was no buildup, no romance, no illusion of something more. Just two people meeting honestly, without expectation.

The connection was intense. Immediate. Physical. But what stayed with me wasn't the sex. It was the moment inside it. A slight tightening in my chest. Not fear, but awareness. A quiet internal signal told me, pay attention.

I listened.

I wasn't chasing connection to feel alive anymore. I could feel the intensity without surrendering to it. Maui had taught me how to listen, not just to the island, but to my own instincts.

And I trusted them.

22

The strange thing about having years of weight lifted off your shoulders is how light you start to feel. And how dangerous that lightness can be.

It was the freest I'd felt in years. Lighter than I remembered being before. Somewhere in that freedom, I started feeling untouchable. Like life had shifted into fast-forward, and I was finally keeping up.

The studio wasn't quiet anymore. Varv started visiting from Honokowai more often. Star came by weekly. The intimacy became regular without titles. Rory was crashing on the floor most nights. Foot traffic picked up quickly. The door was rarely closed.

During my time on Maui, I'd seen plenty of drugs. They were always around, always offered, and almost always declined. That had been a line I didn't feel the need to cross.

Until one night.

I walked up to the studio after work and could hear voices through the door before I even reached it. Laughter. Music. The kind of noise that spills out of a room when the night has already decided what it's going to become.

When I stepped inside, the energy hit me all at once. Deem. Rory. A room full of women I didn't recognize. The air felt electric, chaotic, fast.

Someone gestured toward the table. Deem caught my eye and shook his head slightly. "Not your thing," he said.

He wasn't wrong. It usually wasn't. But that night, something in me didn't hesitate. "I think I'll make an exception," I said.

That night was the beginning of a split I didn't notice forming right away. In the daylight, I was still the same person the island knew. At night, another world was opening.

New faces. Fast money. Doors that stayed open later than they should have.

It didn't happen all at once. It crept in slowly until I realized I had access to things I had never wanted access to before. Substances I'd only ever heard about were suddenly in arms reach. It wasn't something I was proud of. It was just the reality of the environment we'd stepped into.

One evening, someone asked me to step outside and make a quick trade. When I walked through the gate, a guy pulled up on a moped. He looked a few years older than me, nervous, worn down, eyes always scanning. As he stepped off the bike, I looked down at his feet and froze.

He was wearing my red shoes. The same pair that had been stolen when I was sleeping on the beach. I knew instantly. I didn't say anything at first. I felt the old anger rise, sharp and immediate. For a second, I thought about what I wanted to do.

I kept it simple. I told him the shoes were mine and asked him where he got them.

He didn't argue. He told me everything.

While I'd been living on the beach, a young woman struggling with addiction had watched where I hid my bags. One night, she and a couple of others took them. The shoes and some jewelry were traded for drugs not long after.

I told him to keep the shoes.

It wasn't about them anymore. I didn't need them.

Life circles back in strange ways. There wasn't room in me for resentment anymore. I let it go.

It wasn't just sex, drugs, and chaos.

Deem paddled with the Honokowai team. I filmed charity events and projects whenever I could. If something positive was happening, I tried to be part of it.

One morning, Deem asked if I wanted to run a 5K for local kids. If you ran barefoot, sponsors donated extra.

Years earlier, I'd met a woman named Tom while working at the shoe store. She was sponsored and ran in marathons around the country. Ever since meeting her, I'd told myself I'd run at least one in my lifetime.

So, when the opportunity showed up, I said yes.

I prepared hours before the start.

At the starting line, Deem was locked in. He'd decided to run barefoot for the extra donations. I respected it, but I also thought he was insane. When the race started, he disappeared almost instantly. His stride was huge. Within thirty seconds, I lost sight of him.

Adrenaline carried me through the first half.

I wasn't even close to finished, and I already knew I'd feel it the next day.

When I saw the finish line, something switched back on. A second wind pushed me past a few groups of runners. Crossing that line felt like a small but real victory.

While grabbing water, I spotted Deem sitting in the grass surrounded by people, a strange expression on his face. When I walked closer, I saw why.

His feet were covered in blood.

Hot pavement and bare skin had done their work. Blisters had already begun forming, raw and brutal. But he was smiling, proud in the way you are when pain proves you followed through.

I placed in the top twenty-five.

Deem took bronze.

For two guys living like rock stars, we were in surprisingly good shape. The fruit stand had quietly added years to our lives. Coconut water, fresh fruit, and superfoods every day.

No matter how wild things got, our bodies had been built on something real. I felt strong. Healthy. Energized.

He limped for days and never regretted a second of it.

During the 5K, I ran into an old girlfriend from my first months on the island. We caught up near the finish line, sweaty and laughing, and she told me about a job opening where she worked, steady hours, steady income. It sounded almost foreign after months of picking up random shifts.

I applied and got the job.

It turned out to be one of my favorite places I'd ever worked. The shave ice stand was rated the best in the world, and the line stretched to the street from open to close. Rain, shine, slow season, it didn't matter. People showed up. All day, I shaved blocks of ice into bright, sugary mountains for people from every corner of the world. Some days, I met a hundred new faces before sunset.

The crew was just as memorable. The friendships came quickly, and a few of them would last far beyond Maui. One coworker stood out immediately, a woman from Tahiti who spoke French. Everything about her felt different. Her music, her style, the way she carried herself. She was one of the few people who ever genuinely intimidated me.

Meanwhile, the Front Street network grew. Deem and Rory stopped by often, and we continued sending customers back and forth through our underground system. Six months disappeared in a blink.

If someone needed something, people assumed I knew where to point them. That reputation came with perks.

It wasn't glamorous. It was chaotic. Unsustainable. The studio was rarely empty for more than an hour or two. Privacy barely existed. Life blurred together into stories that felt unreal even as they were happening.

Time moved fast. Nights moved faster.

Boogie was one of the last neighbors I got to know.

One day, he knocked on my door asking if I had a little pakalolo. That conversation turned into an invitation, a long talk, and the beginning of a friendship that would change the direction of my life.

23

Boogie lived one floor below me, on the other side of the complex. I passed his door every time I went up or down the stairs. If it was open and that tapestry was hanging in the doorway, all were welcome, no invitation needed. Just step inside. Boogie wasn't just my neighbor. He became my mentor, and, in a strange way, an older version of myself. Antman, he called me.

He was one of the original bad boys, the kind of man whose fingerprints were already on the culture before most people knew where it came from. He had designed logos that appeared on millions of shirts, stickers, and beachwear in the eighties and nineties. Some of the era's biggest brands carried his work. Like, No Fear. He drew the original Bad Boy logo on a napkin in a bar. Just like that. A moment that became a legacy.

Boogie was a man of faith. Scripture was always nearby, and Sundays often meant church. We talked about God often, about using the gifts you're given and putting them into the world without hesitation. He believed deeply that creativity was a responsibility, not just a talent. That you were meant to use it fully and give the work away to the world. He lived by that. But like all of us, he wrestled with his own shadows.

His studio felt like a time capsule. Boxes of old artwork. Sketches from decades ago. Shirts from brands people now call “vintage.” Stories everywhere. Some funny. Some dark. Some are too wild to be fake. We’d sit there for hours painting, talking story, sometimes saying nothing at all, just creating.

It wasn’t just me either. You never knew who might show up. Deem, Varv, Star, neighbors, and sometimes even tourists buying art.

I had always been creative. I won a few art shows growing up. Teachers still had my work hanging in classrooms somewhere. But painting? That had never been my strength.

Boogie made sure I knew it, too. If it was good, he stayed quiet and made me figure out why. Eventually, he started teaching me. Real techniques. Real discipline. I started filming it, not knowing why at the time. It felt important, like something I’d regret not documenting one day.

Boogie still lived off his art. I watched him sell thousands of dollars’ worth of paintings without trying. People didn’t just buy the art, they bought the story, the legend, the man. I watched tourists pay serious money for live paintings. One night, a guy spent a ridiculous amount for Boogie to paint his wife, naked, on his bed. I watched him do it in real time. Perfect control. Perfect confidence. Like his hands were just extensions of instinct.

You could actually live off creativity.

At the same time, I was seeing the other side. The price. The losses. The deals that never paid out. The time taken. The money was spent as fast as it came in. Boogie had once been a wealthy man. Now he was rich in something else. Experience. Wisdom. Stories. And scars.

We were similar in ways that haunted me.

He never stopped moving.
Never stopped partying.
Never really slowed down to set himself up for later.

And neither had I.

The wild part is I wasn't meeting him as a clean observer. I was in it too. Deeper than I'd ever been. That season was the highest I'd ever lived, mentally, physically, and chemically. Most nights, it felt unreal in a laughing kind of way, like there's no way this is real life. But it was.

Looking back now, I can admit something hard.

Sometimes, I was the bad influence.

I started deliberately choosing days of balance. Days of no indulgence. Just discipline. Those days saved me.

Boogie showed me that being an artist didn't make you weak.

I knew I had crossed into real growth the moment he asked to keep one of my pieces. Something I had painted alone. I brought it to him without saying much. He studied it in silence for a long time. Then he told me he wanted it for his personal collection.

That moment shook me.

I had felt exposed showing it. But I felt pride, too. Not ego. Pride. The kind you earn.

I continue to paint because of him. I still apply his techniques, just as he taught me, through patience, honesty, and allowing the work to speak.

Boogie was a future version of me, in another timeline, one where the party never ended.

I learned from him. And at the right moment, I chose a different road.

At the time, I was still living inside that world.

While Boogie showed me what a lifetime of creativity looked like, Deem and I were exploring the edges of the mind in our own way.

Deem and I were deep into meditation, breathwork, and psychedelics. We weren't messing around.

Little Beach was the perfect place for that

Little Beach on a Sunday is its own universe, fire spinners, drummers, painted skin, dancers, wanderers, all of it pulsing like a heartbeat. The only nude beach on Maui, full of light, chaos, and everything in between.

Deem, and I found a spot, and I started small, nibbling on a shroom. The ocean turned gold, the sky softened, and the air felt electric. I floated through the crowd, talking story, swimming, vibing.

As I came out of the water, I heard a voice behind me.

“Aloha.”

I turned and froze.

She was striking. Curly blonde hair lit by the sun, blue eyes, an Australian accent that made everything feel lighter.

“You, okay?” she laughed, catching the look on my face.

“Yeah, sorry,” I said.

She held jars of body paint, wearing a Pakaloha bikini that looked made for her.

“No paint yet? Still in your shorts?” she teased.

“No one’s offered,” I joked.

Then she noticed what was in my hand.

“You eating those alone?”

“Just pacing myself.”

She grinned. “Mind if I join?”

We sat together, painted each other, talked about her surf competition and my life running a fruit stand. We laughed until the sunset turned her skin orange and the whole world felt soft.

Then she stood and reached for my hand.

“Life’s too short,” she said.

We dropped our layers: paint, clothes, fears, hesitation. It wasn’t love. It wasn’t romance. It was two people meeting without asking anything from each other.

Later, under the moon at Windmills, we lay in the truck bed talking about fate, strangers, and how random moments can stitch themselves into forever memories. Then the talking stopped. The silence wasn't awkward; it was full.

By sunrise, we knew exactly what it was and precisely what it wasn't. It mattered because it ended, not because it promised anything.

She wrapped her arms around me.
"Maybe in another life," she whispered. "Maybe we're two turtles or two birds. I'll never forget you."

The next morning, she asked, "If I place, will you give me some Aloha?"

I threw her a shaka, and she understood.

Later, watching her surf, she moved like the ocean had taught her, powerful and effortless. When she placed third, she jumped from the podium down to me. We kissed under a rain of leis. She cried, and I knew why, not sadness, but the weight of a moment that would never happen twice.

"Mahalo," I told her.

That was the last time I saw or talked to her. I didn't chase it or try to turn it into something more than it was.

I carried that version of myself forward, long after the moment was gone.

Paradise isn't always wild nights or psychedelic sunsets. Sometimes it's just showing up barefoot, selling fruit, talking story, and watching another perfect day burn itself into the horizon.

Sometimes paradise is simple.
Sometimes it's just being alive and unafraid.

2016
MANI

24

I was chasing depth. And I was using chemistry to get there. Deem, Rory, and I were microdosing one morning a week, mixing this with that, creating perfect little "functional highs." In reality, we were walking a tightrope.

It was strange seeing people in public and knowing the parts of their lives no one else could see. Watching someone smile at customers during the day and unravel at night. Rich, broke, housed, unhoused, it didn't matter. Drugs didn't check bank accounts.

I knew a server who had been doing well for himself until he started smoking pills. Three a day. Thirty to sixty dollars each. I watched the math destroy him before the drugs did.

I saw a friend relapse after years of being clean. I watched him use. Watched him collapse. Sweat pouring, body rejecting what he craved. For a moment, I thought he might die in front of me.

I had read enough scripture to understand what overindulgence does. Gluttony doesn't just empty your pockets. It drains your health, clarity, and identity.

And yet we told ourselves we were different. That we were balancing it. That we were experimenting, not escaping. The lifestyle is easy to step into. It's stepping out that costs you. We believed we could manage our highs on our own terms.

The truth was, we couldn't. And still... part of me kept going.

There were good connections during that time too. Real ones.

I started filming short videos and taking photos for small local businesses. I didn't charge. I saw it as marketing on both sides, building relationships, not invoices.

The barter system worked that way. Money moved, but respect moved faster. Locals took care of each other in ways I hadn't seen growing up.

I used to tell people back on the mainland how different the kids were in Hawaii. My nephew back home spent his afternoons yelling at an Xbox. Meanwhile, I'd watched two young brothers on Maui catch fish, clean them, and cook dinner on their own before sunset. The contrast was impossible to ignore.

At the shave ice shop, I worked my way in quickly. I showed up, connected with people, and sold the hell out of shave ice. I loved the role I'd been given. Before long, I was being considered for a supervisor position. I knew the system, and I knew how to talk to people.

At that time, I stopped taking new clients on adventures to film. Instead, I focused on friends, returning fruit stand customers, and a small circle of people I trusted. Deem and I made a decision: we were going to experience every activity the island offered until we'd done them all.

Some mornings started in ways that would've shocked the version of me from years earlier. One day, I woke up at six and rode a helicopter around Maui by breakfast, watching the island from above while the ocean stretched endlessly in every direction.

Hard drives filled faster than I could edit.

I started filming a mini-series of my own: *Hempire TV.* Behind-the-scenes life on Maui, marketing, haircuts, cliff dives, business deals, chaos, sunsets, everything. When time allowed, I pieced together footage of Boogie. The idea had been his.

I just held the brush on that one.

The circle started shifting again.

Jerry got offered a promotion that meant moving to Kauai for two years. We went out for one last night together, Jerry, Michael, Mike, and me, wandering Front Street like we had a hundred nights before. Jerry had always been a traveler, never staying in one place for long. A lot of us were like that.

The night after Jerry left, I made a decision that surprised even me.

I started locs.

It wasn't about style. It wasn't about image. I'd been reading about locs for years, their spiritual roots, their symbolism across different cultures, the discipline they represented. Through scripture, through conversations, through my own searching, something about them felt aligned.

It took eight hours.

When I first saw myself in the mirror, I looked wild. Not polished. Not mainstream. People stared. Some approved. Some didn't. It was more reaction than I expected.

But they felt right. They felt like me.

The world has strange ideas about what professionalism looks like. I stopped worrying about that.

Not long after, Varv began preparing to head back to the mainland. During his final days, he cruised Front Street saying goodbye to everyone he'd grown close to. On his last night, we sat at Lahaina Harbor and watched the sun fall into the ocean. A six-pack between us, conversation drifting wherever it wanted.

I recognized the look on his face as he stared out into the blue. The same look I'd had once. When your thoughts feel heavier than words.

That night, he told me more about his life than he ever had before, about growing up houseless, about his mom still living on the streets. You never really know what someone has walked through before they reach you.

Just like that, another chapter of the island was quietly closing.

I started pulling away from the environment I was in. I still went out, still partied, but I stopped participating in that side of things. Something in me had begun stepping back.

I started adventuring solo more often. I wanted to see who I could meet and what I might find on my own. I was watching too many people lose themselves. Too much beauty. Too much potential. Too much waste.

Halloween came again, as time always does. That year was the peak. We had the crew. We knew the spots. I filmed everything, crowds spilling through the streets, gates open, music echoing off the buildings, costumes from every corner of the world. Thousands of people right outside my front door. Parties that lasted until sunrise. Breakfast and mimosas on the beach when the night finally gave up.

It was a night for the books. Then, almost immediately, I felt the drop. The overstimulation. The exhaustion. The tension building in the background. I could feel the chapter closing before it actually ended.

I started seeing past the illusion again.

I couldn't keep surrounding myself with the same environments, the same noise. If I wanted to keep growing, I knew what it meant.

It meant distance.
It meant stepping away.

25

The idea of leaving came before the night death stood in my doorway.

Parties started at breakfast, any excuse, any hour. It was heavy. Everyone knew it. Everyone kept moving anyway.

Rory, Deem, and I were capable of anything when we were focused. That was the dangerous part. When we were locked in, we were hard to touch. Motivated. Creative. Sharp. But when we were in it together, it could spiral just as fast. There are stories from that time that will never make it to paper.

Somewhere inside that noise, a quiet thought started forming. Maybe I should leave before it's too late. Leaving would be difficult. Not because I doubted myself, but because I knew exactly what it would cost.

The ocean.
The night skates through downtown.
The fruit stand rhythm.
The sunsets that burned the skies.
The creative freedom.
The community.

I had climbed the mountain I came to Maui to climb. Not the highest mountain in the world. But the one I needed to conquer. I had become someone different there. Stronger. Clearer. Capable.

I was terrified of losing that version of myself.

If I stayed, I could feel the edge getting closer. I had survived too much to unravel in paradise. But leaving meant walking away from the most alive years of my life. It also meant finding who I had been searching for all those years.

My daughter.

If I stayed on Maui, it would be easy to pretend distance was destiny. Easy to say geography made it impossible. But deep down I knew that wasn't true. Staying meant choosing comfort over confrontation. It meant accepting that I might never know what she looked like now. That she might grow up without ever hearing my side of the story.

I couldn't let the version of me I built die there. I couldn't waste the time, the pain, the growth.

Somewhere deeper than all of it was a fear I didn't say out loud: If I stayed drifting, chasing heat and momentum, I might become my father. Not in personality. In outcome. Older. Broke. With stories but no foundation.

That thought shook me more than anything.

I didn't feel finished with Maui. Not at all. In fact, I felt certain I would return one day. I knew I would walk those same paths again, different, grounded.

But to return the right way, I had to leave the right way. And I hadn't yet figured out how.

Then came the night that turned that quiet knowing into a decision. I got home late, passed Boogie's open door, said a quick Aloha, then went upstairs. I changed, settled in, and then it happened. One puff that nearly killed me.

Without thinking, I grabbed something from the counter and took a hit. When I looked closer, I realized the herbs on the counter were from an earlier "experiment," something potent enough that most people wouldn't touch.

I wasn't afraid of dying. I was afraid of how calm I felt about it. My heart raced, then slowed to nothing. Heat, cold, panic, serenity, my body flipped through every extreme as if it didn't know what dimension it belonged to. Deem watched me, stunned, trying to smoke the remainder to match my level and understand what was happening.

I couldn't talk.
I couldn't think.
I couldn't do anything except surrender.

And that's when she came.
As presence.

Death. Standing in my doorway like she'd been waiting years for me to acknowledge her. The moment I saw her, all my fear disappeared.

Death had never knocked on my door, probably because I always kept it open for her. She would pass by, her gaze brushing against me, sometimes lingering on those I loved. I was afraid of her, yet my anger would mock her, daring her to come closer.
I lay by the open door that night, eyes closed, silently calling

her name. When I opened my eyes, there she was, standing on the lanai. To my surprise, all the fear, anxiety, and pain I had carried vanished. My soul felt calm, as if it had finally found peace.

As the world around me faded into darkness, I closed my eyes and made peace with myself. Moments of my life played like a reel, illuminating my mind and reminding me of who I had been. I felt weightless, suspended in a limbo between here and somewhere else.

Morning light streamed through the doorway. She was gone, leaving me there, alive and unchanged on the outside but profoundly different inside.

That night forced a clarity I couldn't ignore. The island wasn't pushing me out. It was releasing me. I had learned the difference between staying loyal to a place and staying loyal to myself.

People wanted me to stay. Persuasive letters and conversations flooded in.

There was a world I still needed to see. Experiences I hadn't lived yet. And somewhere out there was a small version of me growing up without me. That truth outweighed everything.

No conversation could have delayed it. My direction felt final. I knew who I was. I knew who I wanted to become. Leaving Maui wasn't running away. It was evolution.

Maui had given me everything I came for. Heart, backbone, and soul. The most incredible gift it gave me was simple. I was finally the man my future deserved.

Not perfect.
Not finished.
But whole.

I left Maui with a smile, grateful, proud, at peace, and ready for whatever came next.

Because Maui didn't save me.
It shaped me.

26

I didn't leave.

Not yet.

On the way to the airport, something in me stayed calm instead of urgent. I needed time to process the last five years, everything I'd lived, everything I'd survived, and the versions of myself I had finally begun to understand.

I knew I could go back.

I just wasn't ready yet.

The truth was more complicated than needing time. I loved Maui. I loved the chaos of it. The feeling that the boys and I were holding each other up in the middle of the Pacific. Deem, Rory, the crew. We were brothers out there, and I didn't want to leave that. But sometimes your soul just knows.

So, I made a few calls.

Friends on Kauai answered like they already knew I was coming. I'd heard how people talked about it, quieter, slower, less impressed by noise. *The Garden Isle*. A place where things didn't need to perform.

By the time I reached the airport, I wasn't looking at flights to the mainland anymore. I was booking a one-way ticket to Kauai on the last prop plane of the night.

I landed in Lihue and reached out again. I had options, but I chose Jerry and Jazz. I knew what I was stepping into, and that mattered. They lived deep in Waimea Valley, tucked into a stretch of land that felt untouched by people.

Kauai was immediately different. Lushier. Heavier with greenery. The house sat right against the Waimea River, so deep in the valley we didn't even have a mailbox. Mail was picked up in town.

There weren't many outsiders around. The area was older, quieter, and more local. The beaches were rougher. The water didn't invite you, it warned you. And when I looked out across the ocean, there was nothing but Niihau in the far distance. No neighboring islands. No sense of enclosure. Just open.

My room was upstairs, close to the river. At night, the peacocks climbed their trees and screamed, then again at first light. Then came the water. Then the rest of the valley settling into itself. When I looked up at the Milky Way, it felt like the island was the only thing left in existence.

Sometimes I heard sounds Auntie said were the *Menehune*. I never saw anything. But I felt watched, not threatened, just noticed.

Mornings were simple. Coffee. Papaya picked fresh. I stretched beside the river while the valley woke up around me. No traffic. No voices. Just animals. Peacocks, goats, chickens, geckos, and birds, I didn't know the names of. It felt like a private retreat I hadn't earned but was being allowed to use.

Maui had lit my fire.

Kauai reminded me how to hold it.

When you step out of a party life all at once, your body notices. The first week came with heavy dreams, just reminders that intensity leaves residue. They came in waves, vivid and relentless, sweat-soaked nights when my mind felt as if it were emptying itself.

Then it passed.

A few weeks in, I was clear-headed. Grounded. I took a night job at a small gas station in Kapaa. Overnight shifts. Strange crowds. Forty-five minutes each way through dark, winding roads that felt more meditative than tiring. I worked opposite hours from everyone else, which meant long stretches of being alone, and for once, that felt good.

I wandered the island when I wasn't working. Polihale. Donkey Beach. The North Shore. Once, I followed a guy six miles into the jungle, camped overnight, then hiked another six to a waterfall. Deep inside, we stumbled onto a community of travelers living entirely off the land, over a hundred people, unreachable by vehicles, reachable only by foot and helicopter.

It didn't sit right with me, not because of how they lived, but because of how they treated the *Aina*. Locals stepped in. Police followed. The land was left alone again. And honestly, I was glad.

Life stayed small. I barely skateboarded. Stayed away from TV and radio. Went out occasionally. Sometimes, I'd catch an old film at a small theater. That was enough.

I camped on a Polihale beach, a seventeen-mile stretch of white sand. When I woke before sunrise, the island felt empty in a way I had never experienced before. Just the ocean, the mist, and the light slowly climbing out of the dark. No voices. No houses. No cars. For a moment, it felt like I was the only person left on earth.

And instead of feeling lonely, I felt peaceful.

One day, staring at my reflection, I smiled.

For years, I had imagined a version of myself I hoped I might grow into someday. Standing there on Kauai, I realized something. The man I had been chasing was already there.

The mask was gone, not hidden, and not adjusted. Shattered.

That mask cost me years, opportunities I declined, people I let take advantage of me, and versions of myself I never allowed to emerge because I wasn't present enough to protect them.

I never let anyone get close enough to really know me. I stayed through betrayal because leaving felt lonelier than being unseen. I called it independence. It was just distance dressed up as strength.

Kauai slowed everything down.
River noise at night. No one asking who I used to be. I wasn't alone anymore. I had me.

I learned that family didn't mean blood. That strength didn't mean disappearing to avoid disappointment.

I didn't want validation. I didn't need to be chosen to feel whole. I knew I could choose, consciously and carefully, who was allowed to see me fully.

I no longer wanted a life that ended with just me. I wanted to create something that would leave a lasting impact. I wanted to leave my stamp on time.

Kauai didn't fix me.
It finished the sentence Maui started.

When I left, I wasn't sad. I wasn't clinging. I trusted the ground beneath my feet. I didn't know exactly what was next. But I knew I was ready for whatever life asked of me.

The darkness no longer led the way.

I did.

Epilogue

Years have passed since the islands.

One afternoon, I sat in the bleachers beside my youngest daughter while we watched her big sister play basketball. The gym buzzed with noise, sneakers squeaking across the floor, parents cheering from the stands, whistles echoing off the walls.

At some point, my youngest leaned against me while watching the game. Then I heard it. “I love you.” The two of them hugged and laughed before running off together. For a second, the whole world felt exactly the way it was supposed to.

Moments like that stop me every time. Not because they’re big. Because there was a time in my life I never thought I’d live long enough to experience them.

I live back on the mainland now. I read constantly. I travel when I can. I bought a small home near my daughters; a place I call home base.

Life is simple these days. And after everything, I’ve learned not to underestimate the value of simple.

I watch my oldest growing into the woman she’s becoming. Her younger sister has never known a life without me there. Sometimes I watch them together and think about how impossible this version of my life once felt.

For years, I believed I wasn't capable of stability. That everything I touched eventually fell apart. I thought I was too broken to be loved fully, too lost to become anything steady.

I was wrong.

My daughters know a version of me no one else really sees. They know the kid still living somewhere inside me. The playful side. The curious side. The part of me that survived everything life tried to harden. Somehow, they brought him back to the surface.

I still think about my son often. His presence never left. Sometimes I see him in my daughters. Their eyes, their smiles, certain expressions that stop me before I even understand why. When I look at my oldest, I wonder who he would have become beside her. When I look at my youngest, there are moments where it feels like he's looking back at me through her eyes.

Grief changes shape as time passes. But it never truly leaves. Hawaii didn't erase my pain. It erased the version of me that believed I deserved to stay buried inside it. The islands slowed me down long enough to finally hear myself underneath all the noise.

For most of my life, I worried about what everyone else thought of me. I shaped myself around other people's expectations, trying to become whatever version made me easier to accept.

I wasted years doing that.

Eventually, I realized the person I had abandoned most was myself.

I never knew my father. Never met him. For a long time, I carried a quiet fear that I would become the same kind of absence in someone else's life. Somewhere along the road, that fear became responsibility. Then responsibility became presence. And presence changed everything.

The moment I realized I had truly survived didn't happen in Hawaii. It happened years later at my best friend Jesse's funeral.

Standing there listening to his brother speak, I suddenly felt the full weight of time. Jesse had known me before my life split apart. He knew the reckless version of me, the lost version, the growing version. He saw every stage. Standing there, I realized something I had never fully let myself admit before:

I survived all of it.

Not perfectly.
Not gracefully.

But I survived.

I forgive myself now. For being lost. For spiraling after my son died. For not knowing how to carry grief at nineteen years old. No one is prepared for that kind of loss. I was too hard on myself for too many years.

I understand that now.

Fear never disappeared completely. But I learned something about fear. Fear is often life asking to be paid attention to. And for a long time, I wasn't present enough to listen.

Now I am.

Movies on the couch. Late-night conversations. Sitting in silence with my daughters. Small moments younger versions of me would have rushed right past. Those moments matter more than everything I spent years chasing.

This book exists because I needed proof that change was real. Not sudden change. Not perfect change. Slow change. Painful change. The kind that happens quietly while nobody is looking.

Maui didn't save me. It gave me the space to become someone capable of saving himself.

The nineteen-year-old boy standing in the snow had no idea where life would lead him. But the man writing these words finally understands why he kept going.

He was learning how to become present enough to live.

Uncle Mike

09/29/1962 – 01/25/2026

Mahalo

Glossary

(These words are part of the places and people that shaped this story; they're included here for clarity, not translation.)

Aina (ah-ee-nah) — a crucial Hawaiian concept meaning "land."

Aloha *(ah-LOH-hah)* — Hello, goodbye, love, and a way of showing respect and presence.

Bebadeeze *(beh-bah-DEEZ)* — Underwear.

Cheehoo — Expression of excitement or approval.

Haleakala — (Hah-leh-ah-kah-LAH) — Volcano located on east Maui. The name translates to "House of the Sun."

Haole *(HOW-leh)* — A non-local person; often a white outsider; meaning depends on context and tone.

Hapa — It has evolved into a term of identity for people with mixed ethnic backgrounds. The term is generally not considered derogatory but is instead used as a marker of community and pride.

Howzit / Howz it — How are you? What's going on?

Honu *(HOH-noo)* — Sea turtle; symbol of endurance and guidance.

Jagg — Wild, reckless, chaotic; pushed past normal limits, often from partying or poor decisions.

Lanai *(LAH-nye)* — Porch or balcony.

Mahalo *(mah-HAH-loh)* — Thank you; gratitude.

Mayjah — Major, impressive, excellent, or big deal.

Menehune (meh-neh-HOO-neh) — Mythic Forest dwellers and spiritual guardians of the land; rarely seen, often sensed, tied to the deeper, unseen rhythms of Hawaii.

Nene *(NAY-nay)* — The Hawaiian goose; rare and protected.

Ohana *(oh-HAH-nah)* — Family, including chosen family; responsibility, not just blood.

Ono — Good, good to eat.

Onolicious — Extremely tasty and wonderful. Connection with Ono.

Pakalolo — *(pah-kah-LOH-loh)* — cannabis.

Pali — Cliff.

Pau — (pow) Finished. Done. Completed. Ended.

Shaka *(SHAH-kah)* — A hand gesture meaning aloha, thanks, respect, or "all good," depending on context.

Shoots — Okay; sounds good; understood.

Talk story — To talk casually; to share time and conversation.

Wahine *(wah-HEE-neh)* — Woman.

About the Author

Anthony D. Hemp writes about the moments that break a life open, and the long road that follows.

His work is shaped by lived experience, imagination, and soul. His greatest love is film.

He is the father of two daughters, who continue to shape the way he sees and moves through life.

Salt, Fire & Mango Juice is his first book.

He continues to write and live in a way that gives him something real to say.

www.ingramcontent.com/pod-product-compliance
Lightning Source LLC
LaVergne TN
LVHW010612100826
845148LV00014B/2929

* 9 7 9 8 2 3 4 0 3 2 9 1 1 *